THE GUN CONTROL MOVEMENT

SOCIAL MOVEMENTS PAST AND PRESENT

Robert D. Benford, Editor

THE GUN CONTROL MOVEMENT

Gregg Lee Carter

Twayne Publishers
An Imprint of Simon & Schuster Macmillan
New York

Prentice Hall International
London Mexico City New Delhi Singapore Sydney Toronto

The Gun Control Movement
Gregg Lee Carter

Copyright © 1997 by Twayne Publishers

Twayne Publishers
An Imprint of Simon & Schuster Macmillan
1633 Broadway
New York, NY 10019

Library of Congress Cataloging-in-Publication Data
Carter, Gregg Lee, 1951–
    The gun control movement / Gregg Lee Carter.
        p.   cm. — (Social movements past and present)
    Includes bibliographical references and index.
    ISBN 0-8057-3885-1 (alk. paper)
    1. Gun control—United States—History.   2. Firearms—Law and
legislation—United States—History.   3. Firearms—Social aspects—
United States.   4. Social movements—United States.   I. Title.
II. Series.
HV7436.C37   1997
363.3'3'0973—dc21   97-6371
                                                                                      CIP

10 9 8 7 6 5 4 3 2 1

Printed in the United States of America

Contents

Tables and Figures

Preface

This book is the result of two years of research on gun violence and on groups that have strong sentiments about whether gun violence is, in part, a product of weak gun control laws. It proposes no new or easy solutions to the problem of gun violence, and it is not pro or anti gun control. It does, however, map the social and political landscape of the gun control movement in the United States—the key organizations, their histories, their ideologies, their tactics, their key victories, and their key losses. It also analyzes American attitudes toward gun control and the degree to which these attitudes cohere with the agendas of the key organizations (Handgun Control Incorporated and the National Rifle Association). Further, it compares gun laws and rates of gun violence in this country with those in other countries in an attempt to illuminate the U.S. case with cross-national and historical perspectives.

In writing *The Gun Control Movement,* I studied past research on gun violence, gun control organizations, and popular attitudes on gun control. I interviewed many government officials, many staff members of both high- and low-profile organizations involved in the gun control debate, and many supporters on both the pro- and anticontrol sides. I attended national and regional conferences and listened intently to scholars—mainly sociologists, criminologists, and political scientists—presenting their research on gun-related topics. I analyzed governmental and other survey data related to guns, using multivariable statistical techniques. I shared my findings and interpretations with those colleagues who were willing to act as sounding boards and devil's advocates.

To these traditional research techniques, I added the cutting-edge research tool of the twenty-first century, the Internet and the World Wide Web. I used numerous Gopher servers, Netscape search engines, and *FTP anonymous* as gateways to the world's electronic libraries. What I found was a treasure trove of information—thousands of pages of text, statistics, and graphics on U.S. and international gun violence, gun control legislation, and popular sentiments toward guns. So that other scholars or interested individuals in the general public may verify or further explore my sources, I have tried to reference Internet addresses and file names wherever possible. As of the mid-1990s, I cannot imagine any serious scholar not using the seemingly boundless resources of the Internet to assist his or her research.

Eric Hirsch (Providence College) and Irwin Sanders (*emeritus,* Boston University) were gracious enough to review all five chapters of this book. Irwin Sanders also deserves credit for convincing me in the winter of 1993 that a book on the gun control movement from a sociological perspective was needed and that I was the person who should write it. Through the course of many crucial conversations with Dr. Sanders that winter, I developed the ideas to guide my research.

Without exception, staff members of the Department of Justice, the U.S. Congress, the Library of Congress, the National Rifle Association, the Second Amendment Foundation, the Coalition to Stop Gun Violence, and Handgun Control Incorporated were forthcoming and cooperative in being interviewed and in supplying me with information. I thank all of these people. However, I want to express extra appreciation to the following individuals for their exceptional cooperativeness: Timothy Mooney from the office of Senator John Chafee; Rebecca Knox, Jane Ryan, Yoshi Takeda, Robert J. Walker, and Douglas Weil from Handgun Control Incorporated; Stuart Smith of the Bureau of Justice Statistics, U.S. Department of Justice; and private citizens Mark Borinsky, Jeanne Shields, and Edward O. Welles—all of whom were pioneers in the gun control movement.

My research benefited greatly from the Information Technology and Library divisions at Bryant College. The entire staffs of these two divisions have been helpful, but the following individuals deserve special recognition: in Information Technology—Bob Edwards, Steve Frazier, Raymond Lombardi, David Louton, Karen Renaud, and Michael Thompson; in Library Services—Holly Albanese, Colleen Anderson, Connie Cameron, Patricia Crawford, Tom Magill, Gretchen McLaughlin, and Patricia Sinman. The secretarial staff at Bryant is always helpful. Cleo Lindgren and her student aides performed many valued services, as did my student research assistants Matthew Davies and Sheronda Rochelle. My department chairs, William Hill, John Jolley, and David Lux, were unfailing in their backing of my research and approved several course releases and a sabbatical to allow me the time to do my work. The Bryant administration was also cooperative and supportive, and I especially thank Richard Alberg, Earl Briden, Michael Patterson, Eugene Peterman, and William Trueheart. My editors, Anne Davidson and Robert Benford, were encouraging and enthusiastic from the moment each of them joined Twayne Publishers. Rachel Davis is a peerless copyeditor. On a personal note, I also want to thank my wife, Lisa, and my children, Travis, Kurtis, and Alexis, for their love and forbearance. Of course, none of the individuals noted shoulders responsibility for any factual or analytic errors I commit herein.

I have written this book in the hope that it will stimulate and clarify every reader's thinking on the key issues surrounding the gun control debate and the gun control movement.

Chapter One

Gun Violence and the Gun Control Movement

Several facts about violent crime in America are indisputable. The United States has a high level of violence, it has a large number of guns, and a very high share of its homicides are committed with guns. Further, relative to other industrialized nations, the United States has more violence, more guns per capita, and a higher fraction of its violent acts committed with guns.
—*Gary Kleck, Professor of Criminology, Florida State University*[1]

Ours is a most violent society. The United States rates highest in violence among industrial countries. We have ten times the murder rate of Great Britain. We have eight times the rate of Japan, and five times that of Germany or France. The reason is that when we assault, we assault with guns, and guns kill.
—*James M. Hester, President, Guggenheim Foundation*[2]

We are destroying our future with firearms.
—*David Satcher, Director, Centers for Disease Control*[3]

The debate over gun control is often a war of statistics. What makes the wide use of statistics even more puzzling is that both sides in the debate often invoke the same statistics.
—*James Lindgren and F. E. Zimring,*
Encyclopedia of Crime and Justice[4]

1

Why does the United States lack strict, national gun control laws on par with those in most economically developed countries? Does the absence of strict gun control contribute to gun violence in particular and to violence in general?

These questions stem naturally from cross-national comparisons of gun control laws and rates of gun violence. National gun laws in the United States are weak compared to those of almost all other economically developed, democratic nations, while U.S. gun violence is comparatively high.

The answers to both questions are multifaceted and complex. The first question is manageable and will be answered in this book: By the end of the last chapter, readers will understand why stringent gun laws are difficult to enact in the United States on a national level. However, the second question is more difficult. The average person cannot look at the data and say unequivocally that there is or is not a causal relationship between gun prevalence (X) and violence (Y)—indeed, neither can the average social scientist. The most important data on gun violence will be presented in this chapter, but readers must decide for themselves whether the data reveal that high rates of gun prevalence promote high rates of human destruction.

Although the average person may struggle with issues of causality, those actively involved in the gun control movement—that is, both the proponents and opponents of strict gun laws—have no such dilemma. Both sides have strong beliefs about the data, and these beliefs are intensely at odds. To gun control advocates, the data are stark, gruesome, and causal: Large numbers of firearms afloat in the community generate large numbers of violent crimes, suicides, and accidental deaths. Guns are not just another weapon used in crime or involved in accidents, because assault with a gun, whether inflicted by another or self-inflicted, is many times more likely than any other weapon to result in death or serious injury.[5] However, gun control opponents argue that the United States would be a violent and bloody society with or without the omnipresence of firearms, including handguns and assault rifles.

While it is profoundly difficult to determine which side is correct in its assessment of the gun violence data, it is not difficult to comprehend that these varying assessments lie at the core of the controversy over gun control. That is, those working for the enactment of strong national gun laws are motivated, at heart, by the belief that such laws will reduce violence and save lives. As Handgun Control Incorporated (HCI)—the largest and most important organization sustaining the gun control movement—states in many of its flyers: "Our goal is to enact a comprehensive federal gun control policy to reduce gun violence."[6] Those who oppose such laws dispute this belief. In the words of the National Rifle Association (NRA), the largest and most important organization of the counter social movement battling HCI, "Guns don't kill, people do." In its flyers, the NRA repeatedly stresses that strict national gun laws, especially "registration and licensing," would have no effect on criminal violence, "as criminals, by definition, do not obey laws."[7]

Cross-National Comparisons

The United States has an overall murder rate that is nearly five times higher than the average European nation and more than three times greater than Australia and Canada (see table 1.1). Comparisons of murder-by-gun rates reveal even more dramatic ratios: The U.S. rate of 44.6 is almost 10 times higher than Europe's average of 4.7, and six times the rate of Australia and Canada. Paralleling these dramatic differences in murder rates are similarly pronounced differences in gun prevalence. In the United States, the percentage of households with any type of gun is 48, which is three times greater than for the typical European country (16.2 percent), and twice as high as the rate of Australia and Canada (24.3 percent). Statistical analysis of these data reveals strong correlations between gun prevalence and murder rates (see bottom of table 1.1). For example, the correlation between any-gun prevalence and the overall murder rate is .67, while it is .84 between handgun prevalence and overall murder rate; similarly, the correlation between any-gun prevalence and the rate of murder by gun is .70, whereas it is .89 between handgun prevalence and murder by gun.[8]

As described in table 1.1, most European countries and Canada have strict national-level gun laws that are lacking in the United States (and Australia has strict gun laws at the state level). Most importantly, these countries require that guns be registered, that gun owners be licensed, and that guns be stored and transported with utmost security. To get a license, a potential gun owner must typically pass an exam on gun safety. Also required are comprehensive background checks of individuals seeking to purchase guns, including any histories of criminality or mental incapacity. (Here, the United States is similar—as of 1994, any person seeking to purchase a handgun from a licensed dealer, manufacturer, or importer must wait five business days to allow

TABLE 1.1. **Cross-National Comparisons of Gun Laws, Gun Prevalence, and Gun Violence**

Nation	Per Cap. GDP (U.S. Dollars)[a]	Stringency of Gun Laws[b]	Gun Prevalence (% Households)		Murder Rate per Million	
			Any Gun[c]	Handgun[d]	Overall[e]	By Gun[f]
Australia	20,720	Although there are no uniform gun control laws, state laws are strict: Typically fully automatic weapons are illegal, carriage of concealed weapons is illegal, manufacture and importation of semiautomatic weapons are highly regulated, gun owners must be licensed and pass a written safety test, and handgun ownership is tightly controlled (special permits required, but rarely issued). Registration of firearms is compulsory in some states.	19.6	2.0	19.5	6.6
Belgium	18,040	Strict national gun laws: Rifles and pistols may be obtained only by active members of gun clubs; these weapons must be stored at the club. Shotguns for hunting and target shooting permitted. All firearms must be registered. All shooters must be licensed. Background check for license includes criminal past and alcohol/drug abuse. Automatic, semiautomatic, and assault weapons are all banned. Handgun permits are almost never issued—even security guards are not allowed to carry them. Only police officers and bank carriers can keep handguns at home. All firearms must be kept in a locked place.	16.6	6.0	18.5	8.7
Canada	22,760	Strict national gun laws: To obtain a firearm, an individual must get a Firearms Acquisition Certificate (FAC). FAC applications must be made in person and involve answering many personal questions (criminal	29.1	5.0	26.0	8.4

history, mental problems, alcohol/drug use). Furthermore, two persons must confirm FAC questionnaire answers. There is a 28-day waiting period. Special regulations for handguns include another application for a Restricted Weapon Registration Certificate in addition to the FAC. Handguns are registered and cannot be moved from the place where they are supposed to be kept without special permission; private security guards are not allowed to carry them. Mandatory imprisonment for use of a firearm in the commission of an indictable offense. Assault weapons banned.

Finland	16,140	Strict national gun laws: A buying permit is required to obtain any gun. To acquire a permit, the applicant must have no record of criminal activity or mental instability. Permits are issued only to individuals with "acceptable" purposes (basically either for hunting or membership in a shooting club). Gun owners must demonstrate to the police that they have a safe place to store their firearms (a safe; an armored or alarmed room).	23.2	7.0	29.6	7.4
France	18,670	Strict national gun laws: All firearms must be registered; firearms can be purchased by permit only. Background checks for firearm permits include past criminal activity, mental infirmity, and alcohol abuse. Authorizations to own a handgun are rarely given and must be renewed every five years. Except for military personnel and selected civil servants, no one may carry a handgun.	22.6	6.0	12.5	5.5

5

TABLE 1.1. Continued

Nation	Per Cap. GDP (U.S. Dollars)[a]	Stringency of Gun Laws[b]	Gun Prevalence (% Households) Any Gun[c]	Handgun[d]	Murder Rate per Million Overall[e]	By Gun[f]
Netherlands	17,940	Very strict national gun laws: There is a general prohibition against the possession and carrying of all firearms unless a permit has been granted by the local police chief. Permits are given out sparingly; the applicant normally must belong to a gun club (and gun clubs are difficult to join), have no history of criminal activity or alcohol abuse, and pass a gun safety test. Permits must be renewed yearly. In the home, guns must be kept unloaded in a locked location; guns and ammunition must be kept in separate places.	1.9	0.2	11.8	2.7
Norway	22,170	Strict national gun laws: All guns must be registered and all shooters licensed. License application includes background check on criminal past, drug/alcohol abuse, and mental incapacity. Hunting rifles and shotguns can be obtained easily; hunting is a popular sport enjoyed by more than 300,000 licensed hunters. Handgun permits are only given to active gun club members; handguns may not be carried, even by police (police officers may be authorized to carry a firearm only under dire circumstances). The Norwegian Home Guard has 90,000 members, all of whom keep their military weapons at home; however, weapons must be kept locked and disassembled (a vital part removed). Also, applicants to the Home Guard are strictly screened. All guns stored at home must be locked and have a vital part removed and stored in a separate location.	38.7	4.0	12.1	3.6

Spain	13,120	Very strict national gun laws: Handguns may not be purchased, received, or possessed. No automatic or semiautomatic weapons allowed. Gun club members and hunters must register all rifles and shotguns. All shooters must be licensed. Lengthy background check includes criminal past and mental incapacity. Weapons must be kept in a locked place at home. Police officers carry firearms but normally leave these at the police station after their work shift is complete.	13.1	2.5	13.7	3.8
Switzerland	22,080	The most permissive gun control laws in Europe. Long arms (rifles and shotguns) can be purchased and owned without restriction. Individuals buying handguns from gun dealers must acquire a license, the application for which includes background questions on past personal history of crime, mental instability, and alcohol and drug use; the waiting period to acquire the license averages 30 days. However, private sales between individuals are generally not regulated. The nation's militia system includes 600,000 men between the ages of 20 and 55, all of whom keep either an assault gun or a pistol in the home, along with 60 rounds of ammunition. The 26 cantons individually have varying gun control laws, with the most restrictive being Geneva and Basel, which regulate the carrying of firearms and severely restrict semiautomatic rifles. According to Senior Legal Specialist Edith Palmer of the Law Library of the U.S. Congress, "as a result of increases in gun abuse and of various other domestic and international pressures, Switzerland is planning to abandon its *laissez faire* attitude toward gun control and enact a federal weapons law that … will balance restrictions on private possession and use of guns with respect for the longstanding tradition of an armed citizenry."[g]	27.2[f]	14.0	11.7	4.6

TABLE 1.1. Continued

Nation	Per Cap. GDP (U.S. Dollars)[a]	Stringency of Gun Laws[b]	Gun Prevalence (% Households)		Murder Rate per Million	
			Any Gun[c]	Handgun[d]	Overall[e]	By Gun[f]
United Kingdom[h]	17,980	Very strict national gun laws: All gun owners must have licenses, and all firearms must be registered. Application for a weapons permit must include four photographs of the applicant that must be verified by an independent person of good standing who has personally known the applicant for two years. Successful applicants must have (1) no record of criminal activity, mental instability, or alcohol/drug abuse; (2) a "good reason" to possess (e.g., membership in a gun club, vermin control—defense of home and self are *not* considered good reasons); (3) a secure place to store the firearms (a "British Standard" gun cabinet is made of steel, has a lock, and is located in a hidden part of the residence); and (4) a safe place to do all shooting (e.g., a gun club). All semiautomatic weapons are outlawed. Handguns are a rarity—the police are generally not armed, and only 2,500 officers are trained to carry firearms and do so only as a measure of last resort.				
England/Wales			4.7	0.1	6.7	0.8
Scotland			4.7	0.1	16.3	1.1
United States	25,850	Weak national gun control laws: No national licensing or registration; no national safety test; no limit on the number of weapons purchased. Strict local, county, or state laws regulating the purchase of firearms can be evaded easily by crossing borders. The National Firearms Act of 1934	48.0	29.0	75.9	44.6

and the Federal Firearms Act of 1938 banned sawed-off shotguns and placed taxes and other restrictions on the sale of machine guns and automatic weapons. The Omnibus Crime Control & Safe Streets and the Federal Gun Control Acts of 1968 banned mail-order purchase of firearms and regulated the interstate transportation and importation of guns and ammunition. These acts also banned sales to felons, drug addicts, illegal aliens, and the mentally incompetent but included no enforcement mechanism. The Firearms Owners' Protection Act of 1986 put an outright ban on new sales of machine guns and automatic weapons, as well as on interstate pistol sales. The Undetectable Firearms Act of 1988 banned the manufacture, importation, possession, receipt, and transfer of plastic guns, which are undetectable by metal detectors at security checkpoints in airports and other public places. In 1990, federal law banned the importation of "assault weapons," but did not cut off the importing of semiautomatic rifles. The 1990 Gun-Free School Zones Act prohibited the possession of firearms within 1,000 feet of any school but was overturned by Fifth Circuit Court in 1993—a ruling upheld by the Supreme Court in 1994. The 1993 Brady Handgun Violence Prevention Act requires a waiting period of five days for handgun purchase from licensed gun dealers, manufacturers, or importers and gives local law enforcement officials the opportunity to conduct a criminal record check on the prospective buyer; however, transactions between private parties are not affected by this act. The 1994 Violent Crime Control and Law Enforcement Act banned 19 types of semiautomatic assault weapons, though these same weapons can be possessed legally if purchased before September 13, 1994.

9

TABLE 1.1. Continued

Nation	Per Cap. GDP (U.S. Dollars)[a]	Stringency of Gun Laws[b]	Gun Prevalence (% Households)		Murder Rate per Million	
			Any Gun[c]	Handgun[d]	Overall[e]	By Gun[f]
West[i] Germany	19,660	Very strict national gun laws: A license is required for the private acquisition and possession of all types of handguns and long arms. An additional carrying license is required for anyone wishing to carry a weapon for self-defense, but such licenses are almost never given, even to those in high-risk occupations. Hunters must also be licensed, and they may carry weapons only for hunting purposes. Anyone entitled to carry weapons must have liability insurance. Background checks are extensive and include questions on criminal history, mental problems, and alcohol/drug use. To acquire a license, an applicant must also pass an extensive safety test. All firearms are registered and must be kept locked up, and ammunition must be kept in a separate, locked place. Sales between private parties are highly regulated. With the unification of Germany in 1990, West German law became applicable to what was formerly East Germany, where gun ownership was forbidden for all but the political elite.	8.9	7.0	12.1	2.0

[a]*The World Factbook 1995* (Washington, D.C.: Central Intelligence Agency, 1995); per capita GDPs (gross domestic products) are for 1994.
[b]*Firearms Regulations: A Comparative Study of Selected Foreign Nations—Report for Congress #LL94-8* (Washington, D.C.: Library of Congress Law Library, 1994); also see David B. Kopel, *The Samurai, the Mountie, and the Cowboy: Should America Adopt the Gun Controls of Other Democracies?* (Buffalo, N.Y.: Prometheus Books, 1992). Gun law information for Belgium and Norway provided by embassy officials in Washington, D.C.; for Spain, by the Spanish Ministry of the Interior and the Cuerpo Nacional de Police (National Police Organization)—many thanks to Roger Acosta for his help in translation.

c. Jan J. M. van Dijk, Pat Mayhew, and Martin Killias, *Experiences of Crime across the World: Key Findings from the 1980 International Crime Survey* (Boston: Kluwer Law and Taxation Publishers, 1990); as cited in Martin Killias, "International Correlations between Gun Ownership and Rates of Homicide and Suicide," *Canadian Medical Association Journal* 148 (May 15, 1993): 1723.

d. Jan J. M. van Dijk, Pat Mayhew, and Martin Killias, *Experiences of Crime across the World: Key Findings from the 1980 International Crime Survey*, 2d ed. (Boston: Kluwer Law and Taxation Publishers, 1991), 94.

e. Killias, "International Correlations between Gun Ownership and Rates of Homicide," 1723.

f. Killias excluded military weapons because of restricted access to ammunition; see his discussion, p. 1723.

g. *Firearms Regulations*, p. 183.

h. Northern Ireland omitted because a large proportion of its homicides were due to the civil war. Note that Killias also omits Northern Ireland from his calculation of the correlation between homicide and gun ownership.

i. The correlation matrix for the variables in this table reveals strong positive relationships between gun prevalence (both any gun and handgun) and murder rates (both overall and by gun); all correlations were highly significant ($p < .01$). Some scholars have questioned Killias's exclusion of military weapons from Switzerland's any-gun prevalence datum (see Gary A. Mauser, "Gun Ownership and Crime," *Canadian Medical Association Journal* 149 [December 15, 1993]: 1723–24; also see Gary Kleck, "Gun Ownership and Crime," in the same issue). However, the correlations remained essentially the same with Switzerland excluded.

	Any-Gun Prevalence	Handgun Prevalence	Overall Murder Rate	Murder-by-Gun Rate
Any-Gun Prevalence	1.00			
Handgun Prevalence	.75	1.00		
Overall Murder Rate	.67	.84	1.00	
Murder-by-Gun Rate	.70	.89	.97	1.00

for local law enforcement officials to do a background check.) Of special interest to gun control advocates, because this type of firearm is their chief focus, *handguns* are either outlawed or restricted so severely that ownership is extremely rare in most European countries and Canada; no such prohibition exists on the national level in the United States. This is reflected in the comparatively high percentage of households owning a handgun in the United States (29 percent) and the relatively minuscule percentages elsewhere: 0.1 percent in the United Kingdom, 0.2 percent in the Netherlands, 2 percent in Australia, 2.5 percent in Spain, and 7 percent or less in Belgium, Canada, Finland, France, and Norway.

The striking exception in Europe is Switzerland, which has a laxity in its gun laws comparable to that of the United States and a relatively high percentage of households owning guns. Switzerland is the NRA's favorite example of the maxim "guns don't kill, people do" because it has low murder rates (both overall and by gun). However, gun control advocates are swift to note that Switzerland's population is highly trained in firearm safety and usage because most adult men are members of the national militia. Gun control advocates also point out that "in Switzerland once you use a gun when not in war, you go to prison; [and if you] use a gun for self-defense, you go to prison too."[9]

As we see in the case of Switzerland, oversimplifying when making cross-national comparisons may yield inaccurate data. Many factors other than gun prevalence can affect the level of violence in any particular country. One must maintain an awareness of differences among the nations that could account for violence or the lack thereof—especially degrees of social heterogeneity and solidarity, as well as the level of economic development. For this reason, the countries compared in table 1.1 are similar in their economies (developed/industrial), politics (democratic), and cultures (Western). Further, simplistic pair-wise comparisons should be avoided, since "out of any large number of possible pairings, it is safe to say that at least a few pairs can be found to appear to support either side" of the gun control debate.[10] To wit, a favorite pairing of gun control opponents is Switzerland and Mexico: Because all able-bodied men belong to the Swiss home guard and must possess a firearm, gun prevalence is relatively high in Switzerland, yet gun violence is quite low; conversely, Mexico has a low level of household gun ownership but a relatively high gun violence rate. A favorite pairing for gun control supporters is the United States (high gun ownership/high gun violence) and Japan (low ownership/low violence).

Over-Time Comparisons

Gun-violence rates in the United States are not only high compared to other developed countries but have been rising precipitously in recent years. This trend is starkly revealed in figures 1.1 and 1.2. The percentage of murders committed with a firearm grew steadily between the mid-1980s and the mid-1990s, from 61 percent in 1988 to 70 percent in 1993. Moreover, *handgun* violence increased steeply during the same period: from approximately 589,000 murders, rapes, robberies, and assaults committed with handguns in 1988 to more than 1.1 million in 1993.

It is important to note, however, that the increasing rates of gun violence have not affected all Americans equally. As shown in figures 1.3, 1.4, and 1.5, black males in their teens and early 20s are the most likely to suffer such violence. For example, by 1990, the rate of homicide due to firearms for African-American males in their early 20s was 140.7 per 100,000; the same rate for all individuals in their early 20s was 17.1.

Figure 1.1. Trends in Murder by Firearm in the United States.
Source: FBI Uniform Crime Reports.

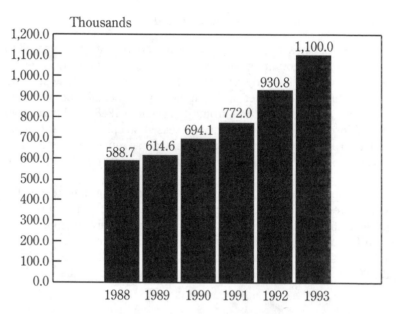

Figure 1.2. Handgun Violence (Murders, Rapes, Robberies, and Assaults) on the Rise, 1988–1993.
Source: Bureau of Justice Statistics, May 15, 1994; July 9, 1995.

Similarly, the rate of homicide due to firearms for African-American teenagers was 105.3, while it was 14.0 for teenagers taken as a whole.[11] All parties involved in the analysis of gun violence—scholars and both opponents and advocates of gun control—view these figures as an enormous calamity in the African-American community. For example, sociologists James D. Wright, Joseph F. Sheley, and M. Dwayne Smith assert that the escalating prevalence and use of guns in underclass neighborhoods have turned these areas into "killing fields."[12] Law professors Robert J. Cottrol and Raymond T. Diamond, both of whom the NRA holds in high esteem, declare that the "black-on-black violence that plagues the mean streets of our inner cities" is "tragic."[13] Josh Sugarmann, head of the Violence Policy Center (an organization dedicated to strict gun control), laments that in many inner-city African-American communities "youth funerals are so commonplace that the dilemma is not facing the question of death, but what to wear."[14]

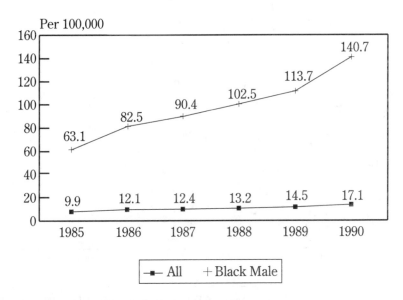

Figure 1.3. Homicide Rate for Ages 20–24 Due to Firearms.
Source: Bureau of Justice Statistics, Sourcebook 1992.

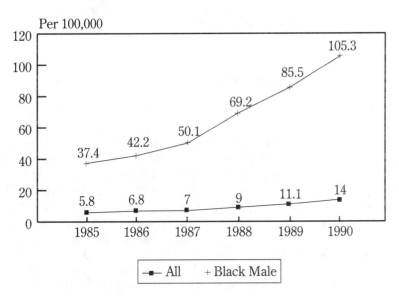

Figure 1.4. Homicide Rate for Ages 15–19 Due to Firearms.
Source: Bureau of Justice Statistics, Sourcebook 1992.

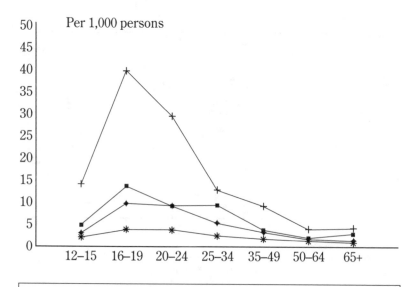

Figure 1.5. Average Annual Rate of Handgun Victimization, 1987–1992.
Source: Bureau of Justice Statistics, NCJ-147004.

But Is the Guns/Violence Relationship Causal?

This question is at the very crux of the controversy between the advocates and opponents of gun control. In the past decade, guns increasingly have invaded the inner cities, suburban communities, schools, and highways of the United States.[15] Concomitantly, these areas have witnessed rising rates of violence. Correlation does not prove causality, however. Several prominent scholars of gun control argue that the causal arrow might very well run the other way, that is, that rising rates of violence prompt citizens to arm themselves.[16] Moreover, simple correlations do not take into consideration other variables that might be determinative of both these variables (implying that the guns/violence correlation is spurious). For example, increasing immigration rates and subsequent rises in violence based on cultural conflict may account for the sudden rise in gun violence. Or, it may be that increasing poverty and the frustration it produces have spawned the rapid rise in violence.[17] Finally, it may be the growing presence of violent youth gangs—springing from low to high levels of salience with the introduction of crack cocaine in many urban areas—that has produced the recent surge in violent crime.[18]

No systematic national-level studies have ruled out these alternate explanations for the recent upsurge in violence.[19] However, it is not unreasonable to hypothesize that the easy availability of guns, both legally and illegally, and their widespread introduction into urban areas during the 1980s greatly magnified the problems of violence associated with cultural conflict, poverty, and street gangs—though some would argue that these forces would produce the same levels of violence even if guns were not on the scene.

The magnification hypothesis is supported when one considers that property crime (larceny, burglary, and auto theft) rates essentially have been flat in the United States since the mid-1980s—most recently falling off slightly (see figure 1.6). This flattening out was predicted

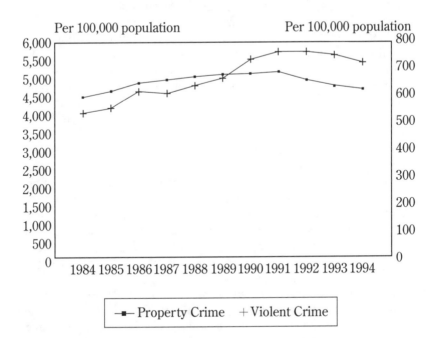

Figure 1.6. Trends in Property Crime Rate and Violent Crime Rate.
Source: FBI Uniform Crime Reports.

long ago by demographers and criminologists, who ascertained that much of the rising crime rate in the 1960s and 1970s was due to the youthfulness of the population. As the post–World War II baby boom generation aged, it was suggested, crime rates would fall (crime is strongly correlated with youth: more than half of all street crime is committed by individuals under 25, with arrests peaking at age 18[20]). If property crime flattened out between 1984 and 1994, why didn't violent crime (robbery, murder, aggravated assault)? The sudden spread of guns into urban areas—their availability, possession, and use—could account for the divergent trends in property crime and violent crime that are apparent in figure 1.6, especially the gap between the two curves that appears after 1988.

At the cross-national level (table 1.1), as noted earlier, one must also consider that the correlation between gun prevalence and violence can be accounted for by other factors; this would throw suspicion on its causal nature. The two most important factors that must be taken into account are social homogeneity and economic inequality. Were the United States as socially and economically homogeneous as, say, Denmark, would its much greater prevalence of guns really matter that much? "A culture in which the citizens are very similar—sharing similar ethnicity, religious beliefs, income levels and values, such as Denmark—is more likely to have laws that represent the wishes and desires of a large majority of its people than is a culture where citizens come from diverse backgrounds and have widely disparate income levels and lifestyles, as in the United States."[21] For this reason, countries with a good deal of homogeneity normally have lower levels of law violation and violence than their heterogeneous counterparts. Kleck presents data in support of the notion that culture rather than gun availability is what best distinguishes the United States from other developed countries that have much lower rates of violent crime. For example, in both Great Britain and Canada—two countries with low gun availability and low homicide rates that are often contrasted with the United States—guns were not restricted in the early part of the twentieth century, yet their homicide rates were still extremely low (12 to 14 times lower than that of the United States).[22]

As in the case of the United States taken by itself, no systematic cross-national studies have been conducted that can rule out these alternate explanations for much greater levels of violence in the United States compared to other economically developed countries. However, it is not unreasonable to hypothesize that the easy availability of guns greatly magnifies the problems of crime and violence that are encouraged by the high levels of social/cultural heterogeneity and economic inequality in the United States.

Further, the magnification hypothesis is supported when one considers the lethal effect that assault by guns produces. Numerous studies confirm that gunshot wounds are much more likely to result in death than wounds inflicted by knife (the weapon generally assumed to be the next most lethal).[23] Although James M. Hester exaggerates in

TABLE 1.2. **Cross-National Comparisons of Assault and Homicide Rates**

Nation	Assault (%)[a]	Ratio of U.S. Assault % to Nation_i Assault %	Ratio of U.S. Murder Rate to Nation_i Murder Rate[b]
Australia	5.2	1.04	3.89
Belgium	2.0	2.70	4.10
Canada	4.0	1.35	2.91
Finland	2.9	1.86	2.56
France	2.0	2.70	6.07
Netherlands	3.4	1.59	6.43
Norway	3.0	1.80	6.27
Spain	2.5	2.16	5.54
Switzerland	1.1	4.90	6.49
United Kingdom			
England/Wales	1.9	2.84	11.32
Scotland	1.8	3.00	4.66
United States	5.4	—	—
West Germany	3.1	1.74	6.27
Average	2.9	2.31	5.54

[a]Jan J. M. van Dijk, Pat Mayhew, and Martin Killias, *Experiences of Crime across the World: Key Findings from the 1980 International Crime Survey* 2d ed. (Boston: Kluwer Law and Taxation Publishers, 1991), 36. Victimization survey was done in 1988. Because the crime survey asked the same question in all countries, the problem of varying official national definitions of *assault* is obviated.

[b]Martin Killias, "International Correlations between Gun Ownership and Rates of Homicide and Suicide," *Canadian Medical Association Journal* 148 (May 15, 1993): 1723.

saying "when we assault, we assault with guns" (only between a quarter and a third of aggravated assaults in the United States involve a firearm[24]), his point that "we assault with guns, and guns kill" is essentially correct: U.S. assault rates are two and a third times greater than those in other developed countries, but U.S. homicide rates are five and a half times greater (see table 1.2). Moreover, although several nations have assault-with-weapon rates on par with that of the United States—of those assaulted, 15 percent were attacked with weapons in the Netherlands and France, 14 percent in Northern Ireland and the United States, and 12 percent in Canada—the homicide rates of those same nations, where the weapon is much less often a gun, are many magnitudes smaller than that of the United States.[25] Such data support the argument that guns transform violent situations into lethal events. Indeed, epidemiologist David Hemenway's analysis of U.S. homicide data led him to conclude that only a small minority of homicides appear to be the planned actions of individuals with a single-minded intention to kill. Most murders involve acquaintances, neighbors, lovers, and family members and are committed in a moment of rage over such matters as love, money, and domestic problems. It is "the presence of a firearm [that] allows a petty argument to end tragically."[26]

Suicides and Accidents

The same disturbing trends apparent in figures 1.1 to 1.5 regarding violent gun crime also exist for youth suicide. The rate of adolescent and young-adult suicide, especially for African-American males, has risen dramatically since the mid-1980s. The overall suicide rate for African-American males under 25 rose 20 percent between 1980 and 1992 (from 8.5 to 10.1 per 100,000). For African-American youths ages 10 to 14, the rate soared 300 percent, from 0.5 to 2.0. Among all 10- to 14-year-olds, the rate increased 120 percent during the same period, from 0.8 to 1.7 per 100,000. The rate for all 15- to 19-year-olds rose 28 percent, from 8.5 to 10.9. Overall, more than 50 percent of those under 25 who kill themselves do so with a gun; and for African-American males the percentage exceeds 70. The Centers for Disease Control analyses of these data emphasize that because of recent increases in gun availability "children have turned to guns to end their lives instead of methods that might fail. While suicides have increased among younger children, suicide attempts have not."[27]

The rise in U.S. gun violence from crime is not mirrored in *overall* gun-related suicides and accidents, even though suicides, in particular, add considerably to the overall total of gun deaths during any one year. Indeed, suicides account for about half of the 40,000 gun deaths that occur annually in the United States as of the mid-1990s, while accidents account for 4 percent and homicides almost all of the rest (about 1 percent of gun fatalities are classified as "unknown provenance").[28] From 1969 to 1993, the rate of fatal gun accidents for all ages fell from 1.2 per 100,000 population per year to 0.6—a decline of 50 percent. The gun accident rate for children under age 14 fell by approximately the same percentage.[29] Although the overall rate of suicide has also been declining slightly in recent years—from 12.8 per 100,000 population in 1988 to 11.4 in 1991, with about three-fifths effected by firearms[30]—gun control proponents argue that "guns add a dimension of harsh finality to suicide attempts."[31] According to this reasoning, "since many of those who attempt suicide do not really want to die, less rapid methods would allow for some of these to be rescued."[32] In short, the unavailability of firearms should result in lower suicide death rates. This logic seems persuasive, and there is no doubt that some suicide attempts that were not truly meant to end in death actually do so when firearms are used, especially when young people are involved.

Nevertheless, the empirical evidence is mixed. At least two U.S. studies, as well as one Canadian and one cross-national study, report a significant positive correlation between gun availability and the rate of suicide.[33] However, two other important studies mitigate the importance one can give the correlation: Analyzing data on 170 U.S. cities, Gary Kleck found that suicide rates do not correlate significantly with the prevalence of gun ownership when controls are made for rates of transiency, alcoholism, and several other factors that are predictive of suicide.[34] And at the cross-national level of analysis, Don B. Kates and his colleagues alert us to the fact that most European nations have suicide rates much higher than that of the United States, even though these same nations have much lower gun availability rates.[35]

The causal nature of the relationship between gun availability and violence is hotly disputed and difficult to ascertain. However, the proponents of gun control are dead certain that the relationship is causal, and they have at heart a simple goal: to reduce gun-related injuries and deaths in the United States through strict, *national* gun control laws on par with those in almost all other economically developed democratic nations (Switzerland being the main exception). The proponents of gun control have faced many difficulties on the way to their few victories. The question that the remainder of this book seeks to answer is why the gun control movement has seen so little success. Why does the United States lack strict national gun control laws?

In Search of Explanations

One obvious potential explanation lies in the Second Amendment, which preserves the right to keep and bear arms. The plausibility of this explanation is considered in chapter 2. A second explanation would seem to lie in American history, which is closely entwined with gun ownership and gun violence. The strength of this factor is assessed in chapter 3. American attitudes and desires might account for a third explanation—that is, weak gun control laws are perhaps what the American people really want. To gauge the power of this answer, public opinion data are analyzed in chapter 4.

Chapter 5 explores a final explanation for the meager success of the gun control movement at the national level. This chapter focuses on the relevant organizations and their role as pressure groups. How do the National Rifle Association and its anti–gun control allies work the political system to achieve their goals? Similarly, how do Handgun Control Incorporated and its pro–gun control allies work the system to achieve their goals? Chapter 5 is guided by social movement theory and shows how changing political opportunities and the various tactics of pro– and anti–gun control organizations have affected the development and variable success of the gun control movement. The natural histories of Brady Bill I (passed in 1993) and Brady Bill II (frustrated in 1994 and in 1995) are outlined. Chapter 5 ends with a summary of what the gun control movement has accomplished—and failed to accomplish—and where the national debate in the United States over gun control is headed in the years to come.

Chapter Two

The Second Amendment

*A well regulated Militia, being necessary to the security of a free State,
the right of the people to keep and bear Arms, shall not be infringed.*
　　　　　　　　—*Second Amendment to the U.S. Constitution*

*There is no reason why all pistols should not be barred to everyone
except the police.*
　　　　　　　　—*William O. Douglas, Supreme Court Justice*[1]

*With regard to handguns ... it is not easy to understand why the Second Amendment, or the notion of liberty, should be viewed as creating
a right to own and carry a weapon that contributes so directly to the
shocking number of murders in the United States.*
　　　　　　　　—*Lewis Powell, Supreme Court Justice*[2]

*As the crime rate grows in the United States and pressures mount for
laws restricting the use of firearms, the need for an understanding of
the development of the "right to bear arms" has increased.*
　　　　　　　　—*John Levin, Legal Scholar*[3]

Can the difficulties and defeats of the modern gun control movement
be attributed to the Second Amendment? This is an important question

because if there is a causal link, then the gun control movement will have little chance for ultimate success unless the Constitution is changed, which is one of the most daunting political endeavors any interest group or social movement can undertake. Constitutional change would have to be the linchpin of any strategies aimed at enacting strict, national firearms regulations—regulations on par with those in most other industrialized democratic countries.

The Proponents of Gun Control and the Second Amendment

Handgun Control Incorporated, the Coalition to Stop Gun Violence, the Violence Policy Center, and other key organizations promoting gun control prominently advertise that no federal court has ever struck down a gun control law as unconstitutional based on the Second Amendment. The U.S. Supreme Court has given at least five judgments bearing on this amendment, while lower federal courts have made more than three dozen rulings. In none of these decisions have the courts ruled that the Constitution guarantees the free and clear right of any individual to own any gun.[4] On the contrary, the courts have consistently decreed that both federal and state governments can restrict who may and may not own a gun and can also regulate the sale, transfer, receipt, possession, and use of specific categories of firearms.

Advocates of gun control like to take the short view of history regarding the Second Amendment. Their favorite starting point is often 1876 (*U.S. v. Cruikshank*) or 1886 (*Presser v. Illinois*), but they are on firmer and more morally comfortable ground when they begin with 1939 (*United States v. Miller*).

In *U.S. v. Cruikshank* (92 U.S. 542, 1876), Louisiana state officials—who happened to be members of the Ku Klux Klan—were challenged for conspiring to disarm a meeting of African Americans. Attorneys for the African Americans argued that the Second Amendment protected the right of all citizens to keep and bear arms. However, the Supreme Court held that the officials had the legal prerogative to disarm them in protection of the common weal. In short, the court held that "bearing arms for a lawful purpose ... is not a right granted by the Constitution." More specifically, the Court ruled that the Second Amendment was not "incorporated," meaning that it only applied to the federal government, not to state governments. The states did not have to honor it, except that they could not prevent citizens belonging to the militia from possessing their own firearms—as long as the firearms were appropriate for use in the militia.

Although this ruling supports their contention that the Second Amendment should pose no barrier to the enactment of strict gun control laws, at least at the state level, many advocates of the gun control movement are not particularly eager to tout *U.S. v. Cruikshank*. First, the ruling is based on an increasingly outdated legal philosophy. The notion that the First Amendment, for example, does not apply to the states is "long gone," and no one would argue thus today[5] (nevertheless, the Supreme Court has yet to "incorporate" the Second Amendment). More importantly, the ruling was racist—providing a justification for keeping former slaves unarmed and in a position of vassalage in the South, thereby partly counteracting the effect of the Emancipation Proclamation. This fact is not lost on many African-American and Jewish jurists, nor on interest groups opposed to gun regulation such as the National Rifle Association. Even though African Americans and Jews generally tend to support strict gun control, some such jurists have contended that regulations on gun possession are a means for suppressing a society's minorities and for allowing unjust rulers to hold sway because they control all weaponry.[6]

There is no denying that totalitarian regimes in the modern era, from fascist to communist, routinely have denied ordinary citizens the right to keep and bear arms. Only the political elite could keep arms in fascist Spain or in communist East Germany and other countries behind the Iron Curtain.[7] And closer to home, so-called "Black Codes" in the post–Civil War South routinely contained statutes such as Mississippi's code that "no freedman, free Negro, or mulatto not in the military service of the United States government, and not licensed so to do by the board of police of his or her county, shall keep or carry firearms of any kind, or ammunition, dirk, or Bowie knife."[8] However, since democracy has entrenched itself in the political system and the culture of the United States over the course of two centuries, it is highly unlikely that the country will witness abuses of its citizens comparable to what occurred in the South after the Civil War and in totalitarian regimes elsewhere in the world. In the present-day United States, advocates of strict gun control emphasize that there are authentic institutionalized means for changing the political system and getting one's concerns aired and remedied. Gun control advocates also argue that even if the fantastically improbable did occur—even if America went totalitarian—ordinary citizens armed with shotguns, deer rifles, 22s, and pistols could not do much in the face of a massive, well-trained, high-tech military.[9]

Presser v. Illinois (116 U.S. 252, 1886) involved the case of Herman Presser, the leader of a German-American labor group called the *Lehr und Wehr Verein* (the Learning and Defense Club), who was arrested for parading the group through downtown Chicago while carrying a sword. More specifically, he was arrested for conducting an "armed military drill," which legally could be done only with a license, under Illinois statutes in force at the time. Presser appealed, invoking the Second Amendment in his defense. The Supreme Court judged against him, citing the *U.S. v. Cruikshank* ruling discussed earlier. Again, the Court contended that the Second Amendment had not been incorporated and could not be foisted upon the individual states. As in the *Cruikshank* ruling, the Court also took the opportunity to reaffirm that the "States cannot ... prohibit the people from keeping and bearing arms, so as to deprive the United States of their rightful resource for maintaining the public security, and disable the people from performing their duty to the General Government." And as was the case with *Cruikshank,* the Supreme Court's decision smacked of bigotry—in this instance, in the repression of exploited immigrant laborers trying to improve their collective lot via unionization.[10]

A more morally and legally defensible starting point for gun control advocates contending that there is no constitutional or other legal basis for disallowing the strict regulation of firearms is *United States v. Miller* (307 U.S. 174, 1939). The Supreme Court ruled that the federal government had the right, which it exercised in the 1934 National Firearms Act, to control the transfer of (and in effect, to require the registration of) certain firearms. More particularly, the sawed-off shotgun, a favorite weapon of gangsters, was deemed unprotected by the Second Amendment. The ruling reads, in part: "In the absence of any evidence tending to show that possession or use of 'shotgun having a barrel of less than eighteen inches in length' at this time has some reasonable relationship to the preservation or efficiency of a well regulated militia, we cannot say that the second amendment guarantees the right to keep and bear such an instrument." Lower-court decisions involving the National Firearms Act and the kindred 1938 Federal Firearms Act used even more direct language. In upholding the National Firearms Act, the district court held in *United States v. Adams* that the Second Amendment "refers to the Militia, a protective force of government; to the collective body and not individual rights." Another district court decision in *United States v. Tot* referred to this ruling in upholding the Federal Firearms Act. Both court decisions made clear that no personal right to own arms existed under the federal Constitution.[11]

However, in its *Miller* ruling, the Supreme Court noted that the writers of the Constitution clearly intended that the states had both the right and the duty to maintain militias and that a "militia comprised all males physically capable of acting in concert for the common defense. ... And, further, that ordinarily when called for service, these men were expected to appear bearing arms supplied by themselves and of the kind in common use at the time.... This implied the general obligation of all adult male inhabitants to possess arms, and with certain exceptions, to cooperate in the work of defense. The possession of arms also implied the possession of ammunition, and authorities paid quite as much attention to the latter as to the former." Thus, the full text of the Supreme Court decision mitigates the impact of its decision on sawed-off shotguns. Such weapons had no place in a militia and were thus not protected, but the general principle of ordinary citizens owning arms and ammunition clearly was preserved.

Gun control advocates are on their strongest ground with more recent Supreme Court decisions. In *Lewis v. United States* (445 U.S. 95, 1980), the Court ruled that the 1968 Gun Control Act's prohibition of felons owning firearms was constitutional. The Court held that "legislative restrictions on the use of firearms do not entrench upon any constitutionally protected liberties." More recently, the Supreme Court has on six occasions made its interpretation of the Second Amendment known by letting stand lower court decisions regarding the regulation of firearms. One of these was *Farmer v. Higgens,* wherein the Eleventh Circuit Court of Appeals denied the plaintiff a license to manufacture a new machine gun, based on the 1986 Firearms Owners' Protection Act, which put an outright ban on new sales of machine guns and automatic weapons. Another was the Seventh Circuit Court of Appeals ruling that the Morton Grove (Illinois) ban on the possession and sale of handguns was within the legal bounds of the Second Amendment. More particularly, the Circuit Court affirmed that "possession of handguns by individuals is not part of the right to keep and bear arms." The Supreme Court refused to hear an appeal of this ruling.

Taking into consideration the entirety of federal court decisions in support of laws regulating firearms, political scientist Robert J. Spitzer concludes that "the desire to treat the Second Amendment as a constitutional touchstone is ... without historical, constitutional, or legal foundation. More problematic, this constant and misplaced invocation of rights only serves to heighten social conflict, cultivate ideological rigidity, and stifle rational policy debate."[12]

The Opponents of Gun Control and the Second Amendment

The National Rifle Association, the Citizens Committee for the Right to Keep and Bear Arms, Gun Owners of America, and other key organizations opposed to gun control prefer to take the long view of history with regard to the Second Amendment. As already noted, Supreme Court decisions between 1876 and 1938 contained language supporting the notion that the framers of the Constitution clearly intended ordinary citizens to possess arms and to be prepared to carry these arms into battle in defense of the state. However, the favorite starting point of gun control opponents is pre-Revolutionary America and even earlier—as far back as Saxon England in the seventh century. For then and thereafter, up through the ratification of the Second Amendment in 1791, various governments clearly intended that individual citizens have both the right *and the duty* to keep and bear firearms.

As early as the seventh century, there is strong evidence of an Anglo-Saxon legal tradition that not only allowed but required all free men (nonserfs) to keep and bear arms: "Every landowner was obliged to keep armor and weapons according to his rank and possessions; these he might neither sell, lend, nor pledge, nor even alienate from his heirs. In order to instruct them in the use of arms, they had their stated times for performing their military exercise; and once in a year, generally in spring, there was a general review of arms throughout each county."[13]

Universal arms bearing for free men continued after the Saxons fell to the Normans in 1066. In 1181, Henry II authored the *Assize of Arms,* requiring all free men (most of whom were landowners) to own weapons: "Whosoever holds one knight's fee shall have a coat of mail, a helmet, a shield, and a lance; and every knight as many.... Every free layman having in chattels [movable property] or rent [land] to the value of 15 marks, shall keep a coat of mail, a helmet and shield and lance. Every free layman who shall have in chattels or rent 10 marks, shall have a habergon [sleeveless armored coat], a chaplet [skullcap] of iron and a lance. Also all burgesses and the whole community of freemen shall have a wambais [leather body armor], a chaplet of iron, and a lance."[14] While continental European society was split between an armed nobility and a disarmed peasantry, in England every free man had to possess and be willing to bear arms.[15]

This Anglo-Saxon tradition was broadened in 1285 with the Statute of Winchester, in which Edward I proclaimed that all men, not just free men, had the legal duty to maintain arms: "It is commanded that ... every man between fifteen years of age and sixty years of age shall be assessed and sworn to armor according to the quantity of their Lands and Goods; that is, to wit, from Fifteen Pounds Lands and Goods Forty Marks, an Hauberke of iron, a sword, a knife, and a horse ... he that hath less than Forty Shillings yearly, shall be sworn to keep Gisarmes [pole-axes], knives, and other less[er] weapons ... and all others that may, shall have Bowes and Arrowes."[16]

During the next 350 years, regulations in England concerning weapons and firearms were revised many times but never denied both the right and necessity of all men to own and be willing to bear arms. However, matters changed abruptly during the English civil war (1639–1689). Charles I, in trying to maintain his status as absolute monarch beholden to no one, least of all to members of the Parliament, began a series of arms seizures from his parliamentarian enemies. To assure that firearms did not fall into the hands of his foes, Charles ordered that gunsmiths produce "a record of all weapons they had manufactured over the past six months together with a list of their purchasers. In the future, they were commanded to report every Saturday night to the ordinance office the number of guns made and sold that week. Carriers throughout the kingdom were required to obtain a license if they wished to transport guns, and all importation of firearms was banned."[17]

In retaliation, Parliament enacted a series of statutes that allowed it to confiscate arms from the citizenry and to deny the right of weaponry possession from those they thought loyal to Charles, including "Papists, and other persons who are voted to be Delinquents by both or either of the Houses of Parliament ... or that have been present with or aiding His Majesty ... or such Clergymen and others that have publicly preached or declared themselves to oppose, disgrace or revile the proceedings of both or either Houses of parliament." From such individuals, Parliament ordered that the "Arms, Ammunition, and Horses fit for Service in the War" were to be seized (*Ordinance of 9 January 1642*).[18] Parliament eventually banned all but the landed elite

from owning firearms. In the Hunting Act of 1671, all persons not owning lands that produced at least 100 pounds in annual rental (which relatively few estates did) were barred from possessing firearms; moreover, those who qualified to own arms were given the power to search
the premises of their tenants and to seize any firearms that might be
found.

During his brief reign, James II, the successor of Charles I, continued the practice of disarming citizens thought disloyal to the monarchy. However, the war between the Crown and Parliament ended with
the Glorious Revolution in 1688 and the ascension of William and
Mary to the throne. Because James II was not dead, but living in exile
in France, William and Mary sought legitimacy from Parliament. After
much debate, Parliament eventually ruled that James's living in exile
was tantamount to his voluntarily having given up the throne; thus, the
monarchy of William and Mary was rightful. The cost for receiving
legitimacy was high, however, and William and Mary were forced to
abide by Parliament's Declaration of Rights. The forerunner of the U.S.
Constitution's Bill of Rights, this document outlined the basic rights of
Englishmen, among which was a clear restoration of the individual
right to keep and bear arms.[19]

The restored Anglo-Saxon tradition of all free men having the right,
and even the duty, to keep and bear arms was transferred to colonial
America, where all the colonies individually passed militia laws that
required universal gun ownership. Hunting was essential to many families, and in light of immediate threats from the French, Dutch, Spanish, and Native Americans, it is not surprising that colonial militia
statutes required that all able-bodied men be armed and trained.[20]
Intellectually, the colonial elite imbibed the writings of Whig political
philosophers, who emphasized decentralized government, fear of a
standing army, and the right of the common people to keep and bear
arms in defense of themselves—against criminals, foreign powers, and
especially the state itself.[21]

Critical in setting the stage for the beginning of the Revolutionary
War were British attempts to disarm the local populations of Massachusetts. Indeed, the first battle at Lexington in April of 1776 was
touched off when a group of local militiamen was approached by
British soldiers trying to enforce the new disarm-the-people policy.
Colonialists bent on independence feared that the British would soon
try to disarm not only the residents of Massachusetts but residents of
the other 12 colonies. Indeed, their fears received confirmation when

Britain's Colonial Undersecretary William Knox circulated to Crown officials the tract "What Is Fit to Be Done with America?" that, among other things, advised that "The Militia Laws should be repealed and none suffered to be re-enacted, & the Arms of all the People should be taken away, ... nor should any Foundery or manufactuary of Arms, Gunpowder, or Warlike Stores, be ever suffered in America, nor should any Gunpowder, Lead, Arms or Ordnance be imported into it without License."[22] As the Revolutionary War got underway, the individual states began to adopt constitutions and bills of rights that were partly shaped by perceived and actual British attempts to disarm Americans.[23] Four states (Pennsylvania, North Carolina, Vermont, and Massachusetts) included the right to bear arms in their formal declarations of rights.

The core issues involved in constitutional debates on the right to bear arms in these four states resurfaced during the U.S. Constitutional Convention's deliberations in 1787 on the need for such a provision, as well as during the First U.S. Congress's debates that eventually led to the Second Amendment in 1789. These basic issues were fear of a standing army and federalism versus states' rights. States' rights advocates, such as Edmund Randolph, emphasized that citizens in new republics should fear standing armies at all costs; these advocates were quick to invoke the historical record between 1767 and 1776 in Massachusetts, where the British army's presence inflamed and abused the local population—and where that standing army tried to weaken the people by disarming them. States' rights advocates were also quick to point to the sorry records of Charles I, Oliver Cromwell, and James II, who used their armies to disarm and tyrannize much of the English populace between 1639 and 1688. The states' rights advocates—also known as the anti-federalists—comprised the overwhelming majority of delegates, but their zeal was tempered by the ineffective governance that existed under the Articles of Confederation (1778–1789), which kept the federal government weak and state governments strong.

Federalists such as Alexander Hamilton were also fearful of standing armies but saw the survival of the United States depending on a strong national government—a government that, among many other things, had its own army and navy. The great compromises between proponents and opponents of federalism were Article I, Section 8, of the Constitution and the Second Amendment of the Bill of Rights. In Article I, Section 8, Congress is granted the power to

- raise and support an army (8.12);
- provide and maintain a navy (8.13);
- call forth the militia to execute the laws of the Union, suppress insurrections, and repel invasions (8.15);
- provide for organizing, arming, and disciplining the militia, and for governing such part of them as may be employed in the service of the United States (8.16).

Concessions to satisfy the anti-federalists included the right of the states to appoint officers to the militia and to train militiamen (according to standards set by Congress). State militias were seen as counteracting forces to the potential might of a standing federal army. Fears of a standing army were further assuaged by giving the civilian Congress control over the military's purse strings and by requiring that the Secretary of War (Defense) be a civilian.[24]

Nagging doubts over the power of the states to maintain and control militias were addressed in the First Congress and eventually alleviated with the passage of the Second Amendment. States' rights advocates wanted to be certain that federal power could not be used to annul state sovereignty. "The aim was to ensure the continued existence of state militias as a military and political counterbalance to the national army, and more broadly to national power (the federalism question)."[25]

However, this was not the only intent of Congress regarding the Second Amendment—which in recent times is difficult to tell because the amendment is worded so sparsely. The spare language was doubtlessly due to the framers' shared understanding of the institutions and convictions behind it. But, in the long run, "these understandings have vanished as brevity and elegance have been achieved at the cost of clarity."[26] Careful analysis of the First Congress's debate over the amendment results in the conclusion that its framers clearly intended the amendment to guarantee the *individual's* right to have arms for self-defense and self-preservation. For example, the First Congress, like its English predecessors, rejected language restricting the people's right only to "the common defence."[27]

How early Americans understood the Second Amendment is captured not only in the historical records of the First Congress but also in how the amendment was announced and interpreted to the citizenry. The *Philadelphia Federal Gazette* and the *Philadelphia Evening Post* of June 18, 1789, in an article reprinted in New York and Boston, explained the Second Amendment as follows: "As civil rulers, not having their duty to the people duly before them, may attempt to tyrannize, and as the military forces which must be occasionally raised to defend our country, might pervert their power to the injury of their fellow-citizens, the people are confirmed ... in their right to keep and bear their private arms."[28]

Finally, the meaning the First Congress intended for the Second Amendment is revealed in its passage of the Militia Act of 1792. The act required all able-bodied men between the ages of 18 and 45 to own a firearm and ammunition and to be willing to put their weapons to use when called on by the federal government. Each man within the specified age range was to

provide himself with a good musket or firelock, a sufficient bayonet and belt, two spare flints, and a knapsack, a pouch with a box therein to contain not less than twenty-four cartridges, suited to the bore of his musket or firelock, each cartridge to contain a proper quantity of powder and ball: or with a good rifle, knapsack, shot-pouch and powder-horn, twenty balls suited to the bore of his rifle, and a quarter of a pound of powder, and shall appear, so armed, accoutred and provided, when called out to exercise, or into service, except, that when called out on company days to exercise only, he may appear without a knapsack. (*Militia Act,* chapter 33, statute 1, pp. 271–74, 1792.)[29]

A perusal of the deliberations of the First Congress on the Militia Act discloses no instance of any representative questioning whether individual citizens had the right to possess a firearm. Rather, the representatives agonized over how well citizens should be armed—fearing that the average citizen could not bear too much cost. One congressman asserted that "as far as the whole body of the people are necessary to the general defence, they ought to be armed; but the law ought not to require more than is necessary; for that would be a just cause of complaint." In response, other legislators argued that those Americans who did not possess arms should have them supplied by the states. Such discussions clearly indicated that the problem perceived by the representatives was how to get arms into the hands of the people, not how to restrict their possession.[30]

Summary and Conclusion

In sum, a dispassionate examination of history and of federal court decisions reveals that there is undeniable constitutional and historical support for the contention that the Second Amendment protects the right of *individuals* to keep and bear arms. This is a fundamental claim of the National Rifle Association and others who are opposed to the strict regulation of firearms. However, the same examination also leads to the conclusion that both state and federal governments[31] can infringe upon the possession (keeping) and carrying (bearing) of arms and that many contemporary legislators and judges have not felt the need to be in lockstep with the full intentions of the framers of the Second Amendment.

More generally, these legislators and judges recognize the significant changes that have occurred in the United States since 1776, when an armed population was critical to the defense of the new nation. In the past 220 years, the standing army has become entrenched in American life, and notions that it is a threat to personal liberty have long been dispelled. The concept of defense being limited to fighting at the borders of one's homeland repelling foreign invaders has been broadened greatly to the point where the defense business of America includes sending soldiers to Europe, Asia, Central America, and Africa; in short, the place of the United States in world affairs has changed dramatically. In the eighteenth century, the protection of the home, the farm, the village, the town, and the city were left to the individual or to the militia; but by the middle of the nineteenth century local police forces were the norm, and by the middle of the twentieth century, national law enforcement agencies (e.g., the FBI, Secret Service, Customs Service, Drug Enforcement Administration, and Immigration and Naturalization Service) were well established. In sum, eighteenth-century notions of the purpose and place of the militia in the community are out of step with the realities of the late twentieth century, and so too, consequently, is the need to assure the keeping and bearing of arms in private hands.[32]

More particularly, the states and the federal government can and do (1) outlaw the possession and transfer of certain categories of firearms (as they have done with machine guns, and as many gun control advocates would like to see done with handguns); (2) deny certain categories of individuals (most notably convicted felons and the mentally incompetent) the right to own firearms; (3) require shooters to be licensed and to have passed a firearms safety examination; and (4) require that certain classes of guns be registered (for example, handguns, as is now the case in 11 states and the District of Columbia[33]). In short, "the Second Amendment poses no obstacle to gun control as it is debated in modern America,"[34] and it cannot account for the difficulties and defeats the modern gun control movement has thus far encountered. The courts have been consistently unwilling to strike down local, state, and federal gun control laws on the basis of the amendment. Indeed, the courts have seldom veered from the decision handed down by the New Jersey Supreme Court that "[t]he Second Amendment, concerning the right of the people to keep and bear arms, was framed in contemplation not of individual rights but of the maintenance of the states' active, organized militias."[35] Furthermore, the courts have ruled that state militias are, for all intents and purposes in the modern era, tantamount to their respective National Guard units.[36]

Chapter Three

Guns in America: The Frontier Legacy

Violence has accompanied virtually every stage and aspect of our national existence ... [and] it has been a determinant of both the form and substance of American life. We have resorted so often to violence that we have long since become a trigger-happy people.
—*Richard Maxwell Brown,*
"Historical Patterns of Violence," Violence in America[1]

The frontier war against the Indians meant that for over two centuries many Americans were armed and ready to kill at a moment's notice. The Indian conflict helped build traditions of individual self-reliance, of violence, and of racism, that remain today.
—*David B. Kopel,* The Samurai, the Mountie, and the Cowboy[2]

The United States was born in blood and violence. It grew to enormous size in part through blood and violence. It has often used blood and violence to handle disputes with other nations, as well as disputes with recalcitrant portions of its own population. And it has a long history of citizens using blood and violence to resolve their conflicts. Some observers believe that these facts account for America's tardiness in adopting gun regulations on par with those of its economically developed counterparts in Europe and elsewhere.[3] In short, we are still too close to our blood-soaked past to entertain seriously the idea of giving up our guns. A number of these same observers argue that, given time, the enactment of strict national gun control laws in the United States will take place almost naturally, as part of the social and cultural evolution that many societies undergo. Moreover, such gun laws will probably occur *after* violence rates have already begun to fall toward the levels of European nations, reflecting a more civilized social order: "People who attribute low violence rates in Europe to banning guns are apparently unaware that low rates *long preceded* the gun bans.... During the nineteenth century in England, for instance, crime fell from its high in the late 1700s to its idyllic low in the early 1900s—yet the only gun control was that police could not carry guns."[4]

This chapter addresses the issue of whether the violence in America's past has produced in its citizens an ardent respect for the keeping and bearing of firearms, and whether this respect, in turn, can account for their unwillingness to enact strict gun regulation. A thorough historical account of gun violence in the United States would need to examine the Civil War, dueling, assassination, mass murder, law enforcement, race riots, agrarian uprisings, and labor violence.[5] However, the present chapter is limited to frontier expansion, where guns have had their greatest salience in American history and therefore their greatest possible effect on the character and sentiments of the American people.

Guns and Frontier Violence in the Colonial Era

In the seventeenth and eighteenth centuries, guns were integral to the expansion of the frontier in all the colonies. Skirmishes with the Native American population were frequent and often brutal. In 1622 and again in 1644 the Powhatan attacked the farms and tiny settlements that had branched out from Jamestown in Virginia. The Powhatan attacks were motivated by what they saw as the greed and selfishness of the English settlers. No amount of compromise for peaceful coexistence seemed workable. At first, every request by the colonists for more land had been granted, but soon the pattern that was to be the hallmark of frontier expansion from the Atlantic to the Pacific became apparent: There was no satisfying the white man.

In both the 1622 and 1644 raids, the colonists were driven back to within the walls of Jamestown, suffering many deaths along the way. The Powhatan sought to make the point as starkly as possible that the newcomers were greedy and selfish and uncompromising. To this end, they mutilated dead colonists' bodies, stuffing dirt in the mouths of some to remind survivors not to "eat up the land," and stuffing bread in the mouths of others to demonstrate that they deserved to "choke to death" because of their voracious appetites for food and land. During the 1622 attack, a third of the colony was killed with its own tools, a message that the newcomers were "working everything to death."[6] For the colonists, this attack revealed the necessity of all men being well armed and ready to assemble into a fighting body—a militia—at a moment's notice.

In 1637, the Pequot and Puritans battled in Connecticut over the same issue, that is, the insatiable land demands of the English. Debilitated by diseases the Europeans had brought to the New World, the Pequot fell victim by the hundreds to Puritan muskets and torches. The final—and most heinous—battle of the war ended when three hundred Pequot men, women, and children were trapped in a makeshift fort near the Rhode Island–Connecticut border. The Puritans burned the fort to the ground, allowing no one to escape the flames. One chronicler of the period describes this event as a "savage and ruthless massacre" that did not fail to convey a harsh message to other native people in the region. After the Pequot War, most Native Americans recognized that the "godly" Puritans "were nothing but greedy, violent thieves."[7] The Pequot never recovered and eventually lost both their land and their wampum trade.

In response to the ever-present and ever-growing encroachments of colonists into their territories, the Wampanoag and Narragansett united under Chief Metacom in 1675 and fought the English in Massachusetts, Connecticut, and Rhode Island. Metacom (whom the English called "King Philip") is reported to have said "tract and tract [of our land] is gone, but a small part of the dominions of my ancestors remains, [and] I am determined not to live till I have no country."[8] Metacom encouraged his warriors to use muskets and to wear English armor as they struck fierce blows against half of the towns of New England—destroying a dozen of these towns and killing one-sixteenth of colonial men of fighting age.[9] The beginning of the end of this war was similar to that of the Pequot war 38 years earlier. Some 350 Narragansett were surrounded by 1,000 colonial militiamen in the Great Swamp near Wickford, Rhode Island. Most of the Native Americans were old men, women, and children. The colonists set the Narragansett camp on fire and used muskets and blunderbusses to shoot down any Narragansett trying to escape the flames. Cotton Mather was delighted that the "BarBikew" had sent so many Indians to hell:

He and other colonial leaders believed the natives were "savages, heathens, barbarians, pagans, and wild beasts."[10]

Defending their land in 1712, the Tuscarora killed dozens of colonists in North Carolina. North Carolina settlers called on their South Carolina counterparts, who sent two expeditionary forces, buttressed by Creeks, and destroyed the Tuscarora—killing most of the men and selling the women and children into slavery. The Tuscarora war was typical of the eighteenth century colonists' pitting of traditional enemies against one another, with the colonists and one tribe fighting that tribe's enemy.

Colonial–Native American battles occurred off and on throughout the eighteenth century. In 1704 in Georgia and South Carolina, James Moore and his fellow colonists enlisted the aid of the Muskogee to wipe out entire villages of Tocoboggan and Apalachee, only to find the Muskogee join the Yamasee in turning on colonial traders in 1715; 90 percent of South Carolina's traders were killed and virtually every border settlement attacked. Only the decision of some well-armed bands of Cherokee to assist the colonists kept South Carolina from being completely reclaimed by the native population.

In the north, as they invaded Native American territory in successive westward movements across Pennsylvania, Scotch–Irish settlers fought constantly with local tribes. These battles culminated in 1763 when the Paxton Boys annihilated entire villages of Conestoga. Further north, Mohawk and English colonists fought often, but other tribal members of the Iroquois Confederation (which included the Mohawk) assisted the New York colonists in keeping the French and their Native American allies at bay. The colonial–Iroquois alliance reached its peak during the bloody Seven Years' War between 1756 and 1763, in which it was pitted against a French alliance with the Shawnee and Delaware. However, by the time of the Revolutionary War, colonials found most of their former Iroquoian allies joining with the British. To the south, the American colonists also found their former Cherokee allies joining the British in an effort the evict the colonists from former Cherokee lands.[11]

In sum, "a state of almost perpetual warfare existed along the frontier, where the jagged teeth of settlement chewed inexorably into the Indians' hunting grounds."[12] And in these wars with the Native Americans during the seventeenth and eighteenth centuries, weaponry was critical to the outcomes of most battles, with the side with the best and most numerous firearms usually victorious. According to some chroniclers, the possession and use of this weaponry on the frontier indelibly influenced the American character: "One may see in these circumstances the roots of the Americans' celebrated self-reliance and individualism, but they serve equally well to explain some of the less attractive elements of the national character. Through the early years, men habitually carried weapons during every waking hour. They became inured to violence [and] to settling disagreements directly and by force."[13]

Guns and Violence during the Revolutionary War

Deftness with firearms, especially the rifle, contributed to the rebel colonists' success against the Red Coats during the battles of the Revolution. The British troops used the Brown Bess, a nonrifled musket that was inaccurate beyond a few dozen yards. In contrast, colonists used the Pennsylvania Rifle, with a bored barrel that imparted a tight spin on the bullet and allowed for accuracy at a far greater distance. Moreover, it could be reloaded faster. This rifle "struck such terror into the hearts of British regulars as to cause George Washington to ask that as many of his troops as possible be dressed in the frontiersman's hunting shirt, since the British thought every such person a complete marksman."[14] According to some historians, "the rifle went a long way to make up for the military inconsistencies and indifferent discipline of American militiamen, and its success helped to instill in the American mind a conviction of the complete superiority of the armed yeoman to the military professional of Europe."[15]

Guns and Frontier Violence in the Nineteenth Century

Through the nineteenth century, in battles with Native Americans, guns continued to be critical at the edges of the frontier. As white Americans pressed westward toward the Mississippi, they fought battles with the Miami, Shawnee, Cherokee, Chickasaw, Choctaw, Sauk, Fox, Seminole, Menominee, Ojibwa, and Winnebago. Crossing the Mississippi, frontier families, militias, and the federal army battled Kickapoo, Comanche, Kiowa, Pueblo, Apache, Navajo, Maidu, Modoc, Sinkyone, Yahi, Nez Perce, Cayus, Flathead, Yakima, Walla Walla, Sioux, Cheyenne, Arapaho, Crow, Gros Ventre, Assiniboine, Arikara, Shoshone, and Ute. As in earlier centuries, the battles were almost always over possession of Native American lands. And as before, treaties made between Native Americans and whites were invariably broken by the latter. Although there were some compassionate whites, the frontier mentality typically viewed Native Americans as a part of the landscape that needed to be cleared away—not unlike the rocks or timber that were removed from the future fields of a farm. Finally, as in earlier centuries, the side with the better and more numerous firearms usually exacted victory: In this case, it was the whites except in the remotest areas of the frontier. For example, in the 1814 battle of Tohopeka, 1,000 Muskogee warriors barricaded themselves near the Tallapoosa River to fight 1,500 whites and 500 Cherokee. Only a third of the Muskogee had firearms, compared to all of the whites and Cherokee, but the Muskogee thought they possessed a sacred power that would shield them from gunfire. They believed that their prophets would make the very earth oppose the attackers. However, rifles and cannon proved more powerful, and the Muskogee tragically "dropped like the fall of leaves. Eighty percent of them died on the fields or in the river trying to escape."[16]

The poignant faith of the Muskogee in their sacred powers was echoed at the end of the nineteenth century when the Plains tribes (Sioux, Arapaho, and Cheyenne) believed that their ghost dance would make their symbol-covered shirts stop bullets. But as happened at Tohopeka, the misguided beliefs of the Hunkpapa Sioux ended in tragedy when two hundred of them were cut down with Hotchkiss guns at Wounded Knee Creek, South Dakota.[17]

In the mid-nineteenth century, the average frontiersman believed that dark-skinned peoples were born inferior and therefore were not entitled to equal protection of the law. As one historian of California put it, "the inhumane treatment of minority groups a century ago in California seems incredible" by today's standards.[18] The killing of Native Americans, Asians, African Americans, Mexicans, and members of several other ethnic groups was almost always done with impunity. Descriptions of these killings are spine chilling. In 1871, ranchers in the Sacramento Valley found a steer that had been wounded by "diggers" (the epithet usually applied to all Native Americans in California, regardless of their tribal origins). The ranchers trailed the Native Americans with dogs and finally cornered them in a cave. The band of 30 included many women and children. The ranch owner saved the children until last because he "couldn't bear to kill them with his 56-calibre Spencer rifle. It tore them up so bad. So he did it with a 38-calibre Smith and Wesson revolver."[19] According to historian Richard Maxwell

Brown, "it is possible that no other factor has exercised a more brutal-izing influence on the American character than the Indian wars.... [T]he slaughter of defenseless women and children, ... along with bru-tal warfare, continued to characterize the white American's dealings with the Indian. The effect on the national character has not been healthy and has done much to implant a tendency of violence."[20]

Gunfighter Nation, Myth versus Reality

By 1890, whites had defeated all of the native tribes, but the culture of frontier violence and the winning of the West with superior firepower was kept alive by Wild West shows and sensationalized dime novels, both of which were popular well into the first quarter of the twentieth century. Buffalo Bill Cody was the subject of more than 1,700 novels between 1869 and 1933.[21] The program accompanying his own Wild West show began with the violence-rationalizing observation "that the bullet is the pioneer of civilization, for it has gone hand in hand with the axe that cleared the forest, and with the family Bible and school book. Deadly as has been its mission in one sense, it has been merciful in another; for without the rifle ball we of America would not be today in the possession of a free and united country, and mighty in our strength."[22]

In reality, though stories of frontier violence were so popular, the level of violence—especially gun violence—in nonfrontier America was but a fraction of that actually occurring on the frontier, which itself was considerably less than that depicted in the Wild West shows and dime novels. From the earliest days in colonial America to the twentieth cen-tury and the modern era, as soon as a frontier area was secured and towns established, violence—especially personal violence—began to recede quickly. The small towns of New England, for example, were essentially peaceful and democratic in the seventeenth and eighteenth centuries. Newly arrived settlers needed the vote of the local residents to become citizens; if accepted, they received house plots and land for cultivation carved from the common holdings. "From the start, the new man was acutely conscious of becoming part of a going social organization and of sharing the privileges and responsibilities that this entailed."[23] In short, the newcomer strove to get along with his or her new neighbors.

Furthermore, as soon as a frontier area was secured and towns established, gun owning and carrying quickly declined. The long gun, the predominant firearm of the colonial era, was suited to field and forest but "had little application in the emerging city. Thus, during the colonial period, the urban areas were relatively free of the consistent use of firearms."[24]

Urban colonists along the eastern seaboard urged their westward-moving counterparts to exercise restraint in dealing with Native Americans, because warfare was a costly drain on the whole citizenry.[25] Those settling in successively developed areas further inland expressed the same sentiment as the borders of the nation were pushed further and further westward. In the larger towns and cities, commerce, banks, and industry were growing. Entrepreneurs feared violence would injure a city's reputation and, consequently, investments. As one St. Louis editor summarized the attitude: "The prosperity of our city, its increase in business, the enhancement in the value of its property ... depend upon the preservation of order."[26]

Of course, burgeoning frontier cities experienced plenty of personal violence, but in the older cities, such behavior was less frequent.[27] Indeed, as one researcher concluded after studying trends in criminal violence in American cities during the unfolding of the nineteenth century: "The existing historical evidence suggests ... that over a long term, urbanization has had a settling, literally a civilizing, effect on the population involved."[28]

It was not that violence was nonexistent in the established metropolitan areas, but it tended to be *group* violence that came in periodic waves in the form of riots and pogroms. Such frays pitted older immigrant groups against more recent arrivals: Protestants against Catholics, Yankees against Irish, African Americans and their white abolitionist friends against the Irish and other whites, Chinese against whites, Mexicans against Anglos. The issues were almost always economic at heart and involved disputes over jobs, turf, and the public largess.[29] Even though some killing did occur, most egregiously during the New York City draft riots in which Irish immigrants ran amuck and murdered dozens of African Americans, the fighting in New York and elsewhere usually involved no guns and often was limited to little more than elbow swinging. Bats, rocks, swords, and fire were the most common weapons. Few industrial workers could afford to buy guns.[30]

Apart from these occasional waves of group violence, urban crime was typically synonymous with personal vice. Newcomers to the city were fearful of the libertine womanizer or tempter, not the armed mugger or rapist.[31] Although guns and violence could be found, they were not the norm. As one social historian of the period between 1800 and 1945 put it, "violence has been the spice, not the meat and potatoes," of American life.[32]

Civility, the Police, and Gun Regulations

In response to the group violence described earlier, American cities began organizing police forces in the 1840s. By the middle of the 1870s, all major cities had professional police forces, and by the century's end so did almost every smaller city.[33] In the last quarter of the nineteenth century, urban police forces were buttressed by state National Guard units, which were formed to help combat the labor violence that was becoming all too common in Northern and Midwestern cities.

The social order provided by these new means of law enforcement was reinforced by public schools, which socialized children to be cooperative and regulative in their behavior. Moreover, adults were subject to the discipline of the factory work shift, which gave them "less time and inclination for drinking and brawling" and other violent behavior.[34]

On the frontier, posses, vigilantes, Anti–Horse Thief Associations, and other such grassroots organizations were the forerunners of police forces and the National Guard. Although these organizations had less than pristine histories (sometimes exacerbating familial, ethnic, and racial hatreds),[35] they were typically dominated by business leaders and landowners seeking to establish order in newly settled areas.[36] And, indeed, in this they were effective: "[T]he vigilante movement was a positive face of the American experience. Many a new frontier community gained order and stability as a result of vigilantism which reconstructed the community structure and values of the old settled areas while dealing effectively with a problem of crime and disorder."[37]

The frontier people's readiness to cooperate for their mutual protection belies the myth of frontier individualism and of the lone pioneer conquering the West with rifle and six-shooter. Eugene Hollon's far-reaching study of frontier violence led him to the conclusion that "most frontier people were friendly, hard working, and fair-minded." For every act of violence Hollon uncovered, "there were thousands of examples of kindness, generosity, and sacrifice. More often than not, people worked together harmoniously for the good of the community." But, as he observed, "these simple virtues, along with hardships and general boredom, do not make good materials for exciting narrative."[38] The pulp fiction writers therefore told a different story.

Hollon documents that the gun violence associated with famous range wars (as in Johnson County, Wyoming, in 1891), gunfighters (including Billy the Kid, Bat Masterson, and Wild Bill Hickok), cattle towns (such as Dodge City and Abilene, Kansas), mining towns (such as Deadwood, South Dakota; Tombstone, Arizona; and Virginia City, Nevada), and stagecoach robberies (of the Butterfield line and of Wells Fargo, for example) was, by and large, the vivid creation of pulp fiction writers.

In fact, on the range, boredom was the word of the day, not violence. There were no newspapers or books to read, no one to talk with, and the nearest town was miles away. In actuality, the famous gunfighters killed far fewer people than the stories suggested. Although allegedly Billy the Kid shot down 21 men, documented killings number only three, "and there were probably no more than three or four more." Bat Masterson was credited with killing between 20 and 30 men in gun-fights, "whereas the actual number was only three." Further, although most mining camps, cow towns, and boomtowns were quite rough in their early days (almost everyone wore sidearms, saloons and brothels abounded, and gun violence was very high),[39] "within a remarkably short time, schools and churches sprang up, and the various 'dens of iniquity' were regulated or put out of business by blue laws." Even in their heydays, towns such as Dodge City, Abilene, Deadwood, Tomb-stone, and Virginia City averaged only one or two killings per year. As for the stagecoach lines, Butterfield, which operated between Missouri and California before the Civil War, "was never stopped by highway-men and it was interfered with only once by a gang of Indians." Wells Fargo and other stage companies that operated between the 1840s and 1880s experienced "relatively few" robberies or casualties at the hands of road agents or hostile Native Americans.[40]

As frontier settlements became civilized, local officials were quick to put controls on guns. Indeed, some 20,000 local, county, and state gun control laws were passed in the nineteenth and early twentieth centuries. As noted in chapter 2, many of these laws were pernicious and aimed at disarming African Americans after the Civil War (saying, for example, that "no freedman, free Negro, or mulatto ... shall keep or carry firearms of any kind"); however, most were striving to protect the public and to maintain law and order. A typical gun law was the

1831 Indiana statute "that every person, not being a traveller, who shall wear or carry any dirk, pistol, sword in a sword-cane, or other dangerous weapon concealed, shall upon conviction thereof, be fined in any sum not exceeding one hundred dollars."[41] Prohibitions against concealed weapons were commonplace by the mid-1800s, as were laws against the discharging of a weapon in public places or within city limits. By the late 1800s, most communities had laws dictating that firearms could not be carried publicly unless one was hunting, taking the weapon for repair, or going to or from a military muster.[42]

With few exceptions, challenges of such laws in the courts were rejected. Most challenges were based on Second Amendment rights either as detailed in the Bill of Rights or as reformulated in various state constitutions. However, the courts routinely ruled along the lines of this 1840 judgment by the Alabama Supreme Court:

A Statute, which, under pretence of *regulating* the manner of bearing arms, amounts to a destruction of the right, or which requires arms to be so borne as to render them wholly useless for the purpose of defence, would be clearly unconstitutional. But a law which is intended merely to promote personal security, and to put down lawless aggression and violence, and to that end inhibits the wearing of certain weapons in such a manner as is calculated to exert an unhappy influence upon the moral feelings of the wearer, by making him less regardfull of the personal security of others, does not come in collision with the constitution.[43]

Summary and Conclusion

Two themes emerge when one takes the long view of the place of guns in American history. First, guns were essential in frontier expansion and conquest, which earned them respect and even adulation from many white Americans—attitudes reflected, for example, in the popularity of dime novels about the Wild West. Second, however, this adulation never overwhelmed the desire of the citizenry for peace and stability. This desire always arose soon after a frontier area was secured. As Ray Allen Billington concluded in his monumental studies of America's westward expansion, the frontier was *not* "a land sunk in barbarism. Those who abandoned civilization were few and uninfluential save in latter-day folklore." He ascertained that "on the outer reaches of the frontier, there occurred a reversion to anti-social behavior. [But] this happened only in the most thinly occupied regions, peopled by hunters, trappers, cattlemen, miners, and squatters."

Among the mass of pioneers, living near their neighbors, no such reversion took place. "When several families settle at the same time and place," noted an observing traveler, "the colonists do not as easily become brutalized as the solitary settler." As the frontier pushed ever westward, the great majority of individuals "carried to their new homes a firm desire to transfer to the West the cultural institutions of the East. They came determined to make no compromise with the environment; they would plant a civilization, complete with schools, churches, literary societies, newspapers, libraries, and a thriving cultural life."[44] Similarly, historian Eugene Hollon sees little connection between the frontier heritage of the United States and its current levels of violence: "Glib generalizations about our bloody heritage do not necessarily explain away our present disorder; [indeed,] ... the Western frontier was a far more civilized, more peaceful, and safer place than American society today."[45]

Gun wielding and violence as features of the American frontier were generally controlled as towns and cities replaced wilderness. Most Americans in the past did not glorify and romanticize guns so much that they were unwilling to support their regulation. Further, historians of frontier America are quick to point out that the idea of our being a "gunfighter nation" is pure myth. Richard Hofstadter's examination of frontier history led him to conclude that the attribution of American violence or Americans' cherishing of guns "to our long frontier history should not be given too much credence ... [because] over the whole course of our history only a small portion of the total American population—and always a decreasing portion—has ever seen or been on a frontier."[46] We can therefore conclude that the role of violence and guns in America's history cannot account for the difficulties and defeats the modern gun control movement has thus far encountered.

Chapter Four

American Attitudes toward Gun Control

> *Would you favor or oppose a law which would require a person to obtain a police permit before he or she could buy a gun?*
> —*General Social Survey*[1]

Have efforts to enact strict gun control thus far fallen short because Americans actually *like* the status quo and *prefer* that guns not be regulated to the degree they are in Europe and almost all other industrialized democracies? The key advocates and opponents of gun control proffer drastically different assessments of Americans' attitudes regarding this issue. According to Handgun Control Incorporated, "80% [of Americans] would support a 'comprehensive' handgun bill, including licensing, registration, regulation of private transfers, a mandatory safety examination, and a limit of only two handgun purchases per year; ... approval [is] just as broad [for] a simple ban on assault weapons."[2] On the other hand, the National Rifle Association contends that "scientific polls have consistently shown that most people oppose costly registration of firearms, oppose giving police power to decide who should own guns, and do not believe that stricter gun laws would prevent criminals from illegally obtaining guns." In short, it is a "myth" that "the majority of Americans favor strict new additional federal gun controls."[3] Moreover, Florida State University criminologist Gary Kleck, one of the NRA's favorite academicians, avers that "most people have no real opinion or only very weak or unstable opinions on specific narrow gun control proposals ... and the few who do have strong stable opinions in the gun control area are mostly anti-control."[4] In this chapter, a dispassionate examination of the data on American attitudes toward gun control will reveal which side of the gun control debate seems closer to the truth.

Do Americans Want Strict Gun Control?

Overall, via local, state, regional, and national surveys, Americans are polled on their attitudes toward guns and gun control several dozen times per year. The results of these polls are fairly consistent from year to year—a strong majority favors gun control laws, and this majority tends to increase slightly every few years.[5] However, Americans are opposed to restricting guns to the degree to which they are in many other industrialized countries—most importantly, they do not think handguns should be banned from private ownership. Variations in the wordings of questions concerning particular subissues do not significantly alter the results. For example, "We should ban all handguns" and "Private individuals should not be allowed to possess handguns" yield approximately the same approval rating—39 percent.[6]

Since 1972, the National Opinion Research Center (NORC) at the University of Chicago has annually polled a random sample of approximately 1,600 adult Americans on a variety of social issues.[7] Along with the decennial census, NORC's General Social Survey (GSS) provides the best data currently available on U.S. social structure, as well as on the attitudes and self-reported behaviors of the population. Because it asks the same question concerning gun control every year, the GSS provides the most important over-time data currently available on this issue: Would you favor or oppose a law which would require a person to obtain a police permit before he or she could buy a gun? Survey results, year by year, reveal a strong and generally increasing tendency toward favoring police permits (see figure 4.1). This implies support for the Brady Handgun Violence Prevention Act, which requires a waiting period of five days for handgun purchase from licensed gun dealers, manufacturers, or importers to give local law enforcement officials the opportunity to conduct a criminal record check on the prospective buyer. Indeed, Gallup, Harris, and other national surveys consistently reveal strong support (85 to 90 percent) for the Brady law, even among gun owners (75 to 80 percent). Finally enacted in November 1993, this law had been opposed vehemently for seven years by the National Rifle Association and its allies.

In their quest to reduce gun violence, proponents of strict gun control would like to see the United States enact *national* regulations on par with those in most other industrialized democracies. Among these regulations are required safety classes (which implies requiring all shooters to be licensed), a ban on all types of assault weapons, a ban on cheap handguns, restriction on the number of guns individuals can buy during a specified period (e.g., limiting gun purchases to one per month), prohibition of minors and violent criminals from buying guns, and requirements that all guns be registered.[8] According to a 1993 Gallup poll (see figure 4.2), the general population strongly supports *all* such regulations and indeed so does the gun-owning population. Only a total ban on handguns does not have majority support. As with the Brady legislation, the NRA and its allies strongly oppose these regulations—except for banning sales to criminals.

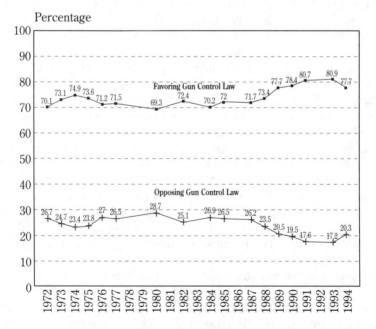

Figure 4.1. Trends in Support for Police Permits to Buy a Gun.
Source: GSS 1972–1994. "Would you favor or oppose a law which would require a person to obtain a police permit before he or she could buy a gun?"

Percentage Who Favor

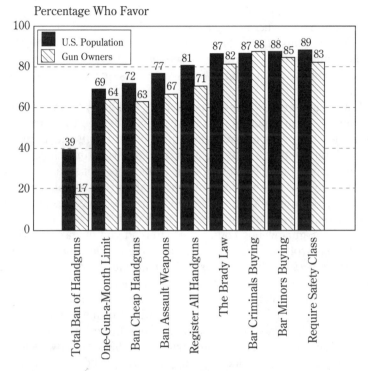

Figure 4.2. How Americans Feel about Gun Control.
Source: Gallup Poll, December 1993. Note: A little less than half of all U.S. households have a gun in the home.

Support for Gun Control and
Social and Economic Background

Regardless of social or economic background, most individuals *favor* gun control—at least in terms of the GSS question concerning the requirement of a police permit to buy a gun. Only hunters (who constitute about 15 percent of the U.S. adult population) do not have an overwhelming majority in support of this gun control measure. But what kinds of people are *especially* likely to favor gun control? The General Social Survey allows us to investigate social and economic characteristics of those surveyed. Most notably, women, city dwellers, foreign-born individuals, political liberals, Democrats, those "afraid to walk in their own neighborhoods," nonhunters, and non–gun owners are significantly more likely to favor gun control than their counterparts (men, country dwellers, native-born individuals, political conservatives, Republicans, those "unafraid to walk in their own neighborhoods," hunters, and gun owners) (see table 4.1). On reflection, none of these findings seems surprising—save those concerning political ideology.

Hunters and gun owners are predictably less likely to favor restrictions on an essential part of their recreational lifestyles (whether hunting in the field or participating in gun club and range shooting) and personal philosophies (the right to use firearms in self-defense). Although a purchase permit by itself is a moderate measure, some gun owners "may fear that passing a moderate measure now would make it easier to pass more objectionable and restrictive measures later."[9] In addition, hunters and gun owners are much more likely than their non-hunting/non–gun-owning counterparts to read gun magazines, where anti–gun control essays abound. Every issue of *The American Rifleman, The American Hunter, Guns and Ammo,* and *Handguns,* for example, contains at least one anti–gun control article.

Men are more likely to have a machismo attraction to weapons. In the words of psychologist Leonard Berkowitz, "for many, guns signify manliness."[10] Men are also much more likely to be hunters and gun owners. The latter applies also to country dwellers. City dwellers, on the other hand, are less likely to be gun owners and hunters; moreover, they are more likely to read about gun violence and to experience it personally, as well as to have heightened fears that guns can fall too easily into the wrong hands (e.g., gang members). Fear of walking in one's own neighborhood is also associated with city dwelling, which in part accounts for its association with support of gun control. Foreign-born individuals are more likely to have been raised in cultures in which firearms are highly regulated and, in turn, are less likely to own guns.

The relationship between political conservativism and opposition to gun control is the most difficult to explain. Philosophically, political conservatives and Republicans are generally against government regulation of individual behavior. In practice, however, liberals are often more unsympathetic to laws that regulate individual behavior. For example, they are less likely than conservatives to support restrictions on abortion, sexual behavior, drug use, free speech, and pornography. But on the gun control issue, the in-practice tendencies of liberals and conservatives are reversed.[11] The conservativism/ anti–gun control

TABLE 4.1. **Social and Economic Correlates of Support for Gun Control**

Characteristic	*Percent in Favor of Requiring a Police Permit to Buy a Gun*	*Correlation (Gamma*)*	*Statistical Significance*
Gender			
Male	72.7	0.44	<0.001
Female	87.1		
Race			
White	79.9	0.16	<0.009
Black	84.5		
Age			
18–39	80.7	0.02	>0.538
40–59	80.0		
60+	82.1		
Family Income per Year			
Less than $20,000	81.0	0.02	>0.535
$20,000–$50,000	80.1		
More Than $50,000	82.3		
Occupational Prestige			
Lowest quartile	80.8	0.07	<0.027
Second quartile	77.6		
Third quartile	80.3		
Highest quartile	84.6		
Education			
Less than high school	79.9	0.10	<0.002
High school	79.3		
Junior college	80.3		
College degree	84.2		
Graduate degree	87.0		
Urbanization			
Rural	69.5	0.19	<0.001
Small town	77.0		
Suburb	81.7		
City	83.7		

continued

TABLE 4.1. **Continued**

Characteristic	Percent in Favor of Requiring a Police Permit to Buy a Gun	Correlation (Gamma*)	Statistical Significance
Region			
Northeast	85.6	−0.12	<0.001
Midwest	81.0		
South	78.0		
Far west	78.8		
Foreign-born?			
No	80.4	−0.21	<0.006
Yes	86.4		
Political views			
Liberal	87.0	−0.25	<0.001
Moderate	81.6		
Conservative	75.4		
Political party			
Democrat	84.9	−0.19	<0.001
Republican	76.5		
Independent	79.3		
Burglarized in past year?			
No	81.5	−0.04	>0.688
Yes	80.2		
Robbed in past year?			
No	81.3	0.19	>0.201
Yes	86.5		
Fears walking in own neighborhood?			
No	77.1	0.26	<0.001
Yes	85.2		
Hunter?			
No	86.2	−0.69	<0.001
Yes	53.3		
Gun-owning household?			
No	88.9	−0.55	<0.001
Yes	70.1		

relationship is partly accounted for by the positive associations between conservativism and gun owning and between conservativism and hunting.[12] However, even controlling for gun owning and being a hunter, conservatives are more likely to oppose gun control.[13] The relationship that remains after controls for gun ownership and hunting can be accounted for by the tremendous financial support that conservative politicians receive from the NRA and its allies (see chapter 5). Of course, the writings and speeches of such politicians help to define conservativism in the minds of everyday citizens.

While attitudes toward gun control tend to vary somewhat with the previously discussed social-background characteristics, they do *not* vary significantly with age or income (see table 4.1). The GSS survey finds essentially equal support for gun control among all ages and all income groups. Erich Goode has observed that "just about all aspects of our lives—from the newspapers we read to the ways we make love, from the food we eat to our political ideology and behavior—are either correlated or causally connected with socioeconomic statuses."[14] But not here. Goode also observes that "aging generates attitudes."[15] But again not here. That support for gun control cuts across the lines of both social class and age bodes well for the future of the gun control movement (see chapter 5).[16]

Interestingly, and of great importance to the future direction of the gun control movement, combinations of characteristics displayed in

---

Notes to Table 4.1

* As noted in chapter 1, note 8, correlations are used to summarize the strength of the relationship between two variables and can vary between –1 and +1. *Gamma* is a particular type of correlational statistic that is appropriate for many survey variables (including, for example, questions on how strong or weak an individual's attitude is). As gamma approaches zero, the relationship becomes increasingly less significant. As gamma approaches either –1 or +1, the relationship becomes increasingly stronger. The sign (+ or –) of the coefficient indicates only the direction of the relationship, not its strength. Thus, a gamma between X and Y of –.5 and a gamma between X and Z of +.5 are equal in strength. The sign merely denotes the direction of the relationship. For positive relationships, the variables are changing in the same direction (e.g., increases in one variable are associated with increases in the other variable). For negative relationships, the variables are changing in opposite directions (e.g., increases in one variable are associated with decreases in the other variable). For an elementary discussion of gamma, see, for example, Michael Malec, *Essential Statistics for Social Research,* 2d ed. (Boulder, Colo.: Westview Press, 1993), chapter 10.

Percentage

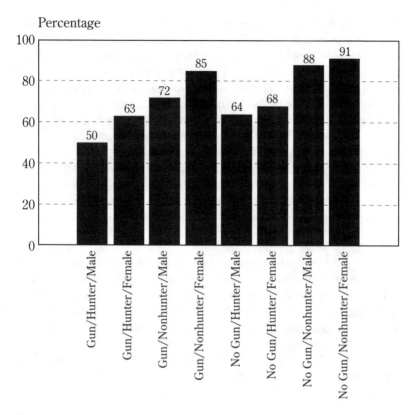

Figure 4.3. Support for Gun Control and Gun Ownership/Hunting/Gender.
Source: Cumulated General Social Surveys, 1991–1994.

table 4.1 cannot be created that would push support for gun control below the 50 percent level. Various combinations of three of the strongest predictors of the gun control question (gun ownership, hunting, and gender) are displayed in figure 4.3. Although non–gun-owning, nonhunting women are much more likely to respond that they favor police permits (the GSS gun control question), half of gun-owning men who hunt are also in favor of permits. Table 4.2 presents a similar analysis for gun ownership, urbanization, political views, and gender—the four strongest correlates of support for gun control (because hunters constitute such a minority of the population, this characteristic is not included). Again, we find that even though the various combinations of social-background traits explain much of the variability in support for gun control, no combination pushes support below 50 percent.

Based on a review of past research, as well as on current findings from the General Social Surveys,[17] the heuristic model in figure 4.4 summarizes the relationships between social-background characteristics and attitude toward gun control. Multivariable statistical tests of

TABLE 4.2. **Support for Gun Control and Gun Ownership/ Urbanization/Political Views/Gender**

Gun Owner?	Urbanization	Political Views	Gender	*Percentage in Favor of Requiring a Police Permit to Buy a Gun*
No	Rural-Town	Liberal	Male	93.1
No	Rural-Town	Liberal	Female	87.8
No	Rural-Town	Moderate	Male	78.8
No	Rural-Town	Moderate	Female	88.8
No	Rural-Town	Conservative	Male	77.8
No	Rural-Town	Conservative	Female	87.0
Yes	Rural-Town	Liberal	Male	69.6
Yes	Rural-Town	Liberal	Female	79.2
Yes	Rural-Town	Moderate	Male	52.8
Yes	Rural-Town	Moderate	Female	76.5
Yes	Rural-Town	Conservative	Male	57.9
Yes	Rural-Town	Conservative	Female	76.3
No	Suburb-City	Liberal	Male	91.1
No	Suburb-City	Liberal	Female	93.4
No	Suburb-City	Moderate	Male	88.0
No	Suburb-City	Moderate	Female	91.5
No	Suburb-City	Conservative	Male	79.9
No	Suburb-City	Conservative	Female	87.2
Yes	Suburb-City	Liberal	Male	74.2
Yes	Suburb-City	Liberal	Female	83.3
Yes	Suburb-City	Moderate	Male	61.2
Yes	Suburb-City	Moderate	Female	87.0
Yes	Suburb-City	Conservative	Male	57.6
Yes	Suburb-City	Conservative	Female	75.0

Source: Cumulated General Social Surveys, 1991–1994. $N = 3,988$.

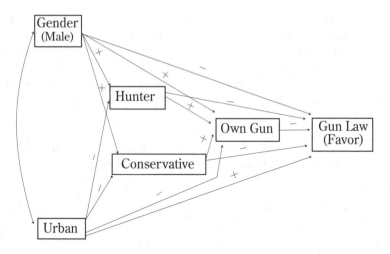

Figure 4.4. Heuristic Model of Favorableness toward Gun Control.

the model reveal that the five independent variables significantly predict whether an individual favors or opposes gun control in terms of the GSS question.[18] Rural, conservative, gun-owning men who hunt are most likely to oppose gun control, whereas city-dwelling, liberal, non–gun-owning women who do not hunt are most likely to favor gun control. Figure 4.4 traces both the direct and indirect pathways by which these five factors determine an individual's attitude toward gun control. As noted earlier, for example, the tendency of men to display more machismo reduces their tendency to support gun control (the direct effect), while men's greater probabilities of being conservative, of participating in hunting, and of owning guns produce the indirect effects of gender on attitudes toward gun control.[19]

But How Serious Are Pro–Gun Control Attitudes?

Because the NRA's position is generally not supported by public-opinion polls, the organization has a tendency to repudiate them: "Polls can be slanted by carefully worded questions to achieve any desired outcome. It is a fact that most people do not know what laws currently exist; thus, it is meaningless to assert that people favor 'stricter' laws when they do not know how 'strict' the laws are in the first place."[20]

Indeed, instead of looking to polls to gauge the feelings of the general population, the NRA argues that "a more direct measure of the public's attitude on 'gun control' comes when the electorate has a chance to speak on the issue. Public-opinion polls do not form public policy, but individual actions by hundreds of thousands of citizens do" (via voting down gun regulation proposals, as has happened in a few states and localities during the past several years).[21] Similarly, criminologist Gary Kleck, a scholar the NRA favors highly, argues that

The survey-based support for gun control may be less substantial than it appears.... Sometimes, a survey "opinion" is little more than a response given on the spur-of-the-moment to a stranger who calls unannounced at the respondent's door or on the telephone, and asks a question about a topic to which the R[espondent] has given little thought. [In short,] ... the appearance of support for [gun control] can be created by the simple fact that most people will provide an opinion if asked, regardless of whether or not they had a well-formed, stable, or strongly held opinion on the issue before they were interviewed.[22]

Kleck overstates his case, however, because according to data from the 1984 General Social Survey (the last GSS to investigate this) the public is actually better informed and much more concerned about gun control than he suggests. When asked "How much information do you have about the gun control issue?" only one in five respondents answered "very little." Most respondents claimed to have at least "some" information and a third reported having "most" or "all" (figure 4.5). When asked "How important is the gun control issue to you?" most respondents (70 percent) said that it was either an "important" issue or "one of the most important" issues to them (figure 4.6). This finding is consistent with that of Schuman and Presser, who asked a random sample of adult Americans the following: "Compared with how you feel on other public issues, are your feelings about permits for guns: extremely strong, very strong, fairly strong, or not strong at all?" More than 80 percent responded between "fairly strong" and "extremely strong," leaving fewer than 20 percent to answer "not strong at all."[23]

Of critical importance to the ultimate success of the gun control movement is whether those in favor of gun control hold their beliefs as strongly as those opposed to gun control. One of Schuman and Presser's findings could be interpreted as showing that gun control

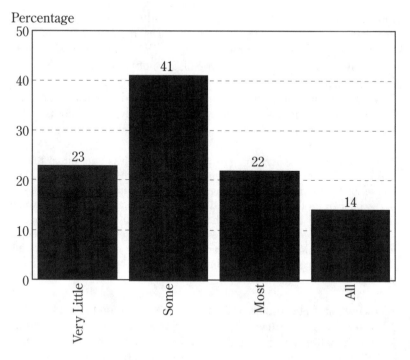

Figure 4.5. "How Much Information Do You Have about the Gun Control Issue?" *Source:* GSS, 1984. *N* = 476.

advocates are not as adamant as gun control opponents. Asked if they have done anything tangible in support of their beliefs, opponents were three times more likely than proponents of control to report writing letters to public officials or donating money to a group representing their interests.[24] However, Schuman and Presser do not interpret this finding as evidence that gun control opponents hold their beliefs more solidly than gun control supporters. Rather, they hypothesize that opponents were more likely to act on their beliefs because of "the efficiency of the National Rifle Association in mobilizing supporters"[25] (an issue discussed in the next chapter). Kleck rejects this conclusion because only a fraction of the respondents could possibly belong to the NRA.[26] Whatever the exact explanation of gun control opponents' greater activism, however, Schuman and Presser's idea that opponents do not hold their beliefs more strongly than supporters is corroborated by the GSS data, since those who favor gun control are significantly

Percentage

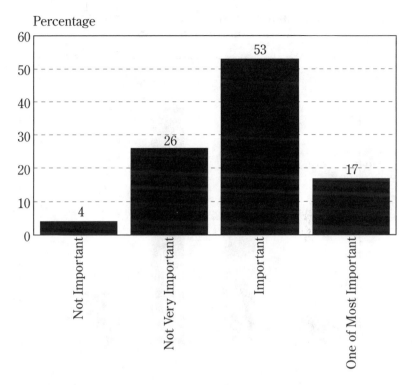

Figure 4.6. "How Important Is the Gun Control Issue to You?"
Source: GSS, 1984. *N* = 474.

more likely to report that the issue is "one of the most important" to them (see table 4.3).

Summary and Conclusion

Do Americans want strict gun control? On balance the answer is yes. Americans strongly believe in background checks, police permits, the registration of firearms, and keeping guns out of the hands of criminals and minors, as public-opinion polls have repeatedly shown. Because the NRA's anti–gun control position is generally not supported by public-opinion polls, the organization has a tendency to discount them—indeed, to label them "meaningless."[27] However, the proponents of gun

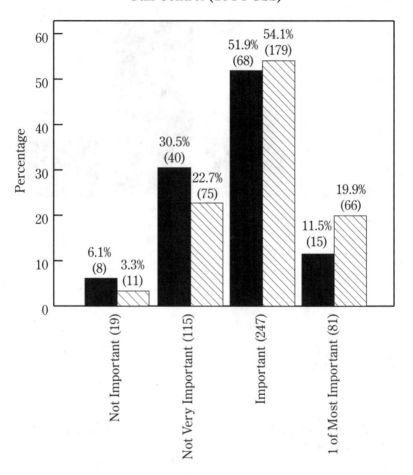

TABLE 4.3. **Attitude toward Gun Law and Importance of Gun Control (1984 GSS)**

Importance of Gun Control and Column Sum

■ Oppose (131) ◫ Favor (331)

$(x^2=8.05, p<.05; \text{gamma}=.24, p<.005)$

control view the situation differently. They see the nation's lack of strict gun control regulations as evidence that the will of the people is being thwarted. In short, they see the federal government acting out of step with the wishes of the people.

Recent history offers us many instances of the government acting contrary to popular opinion. For example, the 1994 invasion of Haiti by U.S. troops was preceded by national opinion polls showing that only 18 percent of the population would support such an invasion.[28] Similarly, the 1995–1996 deployment of U.S. troops in Bosnia-Herzegovina was preceded by opinion polls showing only 30 percent of the population favoring the move.[29]

What can explain the people's will not being acted on with regard to gun control? This question is magnified by the findings of chapters 2 and 3, which revealed that strong gun control legislation is not being impeded by the Second Amendment and should not be hindered by the legacy of the role of guns in American history. The next chapter answers this complex question.

Chapter Five

Society, Politics, and the Gun Control Movement

Outside interests, particularly the president and pressure groups, exercise excessive influence over Congress, preventing the legislators from applying independent judgment about the programs that the national interest seems to require.

—*Leroy N. Rieselbach,*
Professor of Political Science, Indiana University[1]

It can be very difficult for a controversial piece of legislation to pass the U.S. Congress. There are many, many ways for the pistol lobby to derail any handgun control bill.
—*Pete Shields, Former Chair of Handgun Control Incorporated*[2]

The existence of the National Rifle Association is the greatest single reason why the United States has not adopted the types of firearms restrictions which are common in many countries.
—*Edward F. Leddy,* Magnum Force Lobby[3]

The truth is that the NRA's power in the electoral ring has always been exaggerated—its record is spotty.
—*Osha Gray Davidson,* Under Fire[4]

People get emotional about this issue and there's no way you can persuade those on opposite sides to the contrary.
—*U.S. House Representative Harold Volkmer*[5]

I've learned one thing: you can't take on the gun lobby with good will.
—*U.S. House Representative Abner Mikva*[6]

In the preceding chapters, it has been argued that the sparse success of the gun control movement in the United States, as reflected in the weakness of the nation's gun laws compared to those of other industrialized democracies, cannot be accounted for by the Second Amendment, the role of guns in the nation's history, or the attitudes and desires of its citizenry. In this chapter, a final explanation is sought in congressional and pressure group politics. The nature and characteristics of the modern gun control movement, which dates back to the mid-1970s with the formation of Handgun Control Incorporated (HCI), are contrasted with the nature and characteristics of the countermovement, whose principal organizational leader is the National Rifle Association (NRA). Differences in these opposing movements' political opportunities and tactics may be responsible for their differential successes. At any one time, such variances can account for success or failure over a particular battle (e.g., over the passage of the Brady Handgun Control Bill); moreover, as these differences change over time, the probabilities of success for each side also change.

Social-Movement Theory

A *social movement* entails many individuals working in unison to promote or prevent change in society. That individuals work together implies leadership and organization. Social-movement theory seeks to explain the emergence, sustainment, and outcomes of any particular movement or related set of movements. The key constructs that social movement theorists have thus far found most explanatory are diagrammed in the heuristic models in figures 5.1 (see page 70), 5.2 (see page 92), and 5.3 (see page 98). These models display the complex web of forces involved at the macro (societal), micro (individual), and medial (organizational) levels of analysis. They also reveal many (but not all) of the key relationships among the variables at each level (if all were shown, the figures would look like jumbled balls of spaghetti).

Overall, we may observe that medial-level variables connect macro-level structural opportunities with individual-level propensities to generate a social movement. Many social-movement theorists contend that the key to understanding the emergence, sustainment, and outcomes of a movement is found at the medial level of analysis.[7]

We will repeatedly refer to these models in the following sections in analyzing how the gun control movement arose and was able to achieve its two major successes thus far—passage of the 1993 Brady Handgun Control Law and the banning of new sales of selected assault rifles as part of the 1994 Violent Crime Control and Law Enforcement Act—as well as how the gun control movement has been thwarted from further success by the countermovement led by the NRA. We start with a look back at the historical roots of the NRA's anti–gun control position. Following this, we will assess the political opportunities, growth, and tactics of both sides. The chapter closes with predictions about the future of the gun control debate as it is played out against the backdrop of American society and politics.

Historical Roots of the NRA's Anti–Gun Control Position

Founded in 1871, the NRA in its early years was a relatively small shooting association that sponsored rifle matches and sharpshooter classes. It was the darling of the Department of the Army, whose leaders viewed the NRA as helping to keep the general population militia ready. As part of this task, the NRA was commissioned to train members of the New York National Guard to shoot well. However, its state funding was cut off in 1879, and the organization fell into disarray. It was revived in 1903, when Congress created the National Board for the Promotion of Rifle Practice (NBPRP) to promote civilian rifle practice (another attempt by the military to ensure that civilians were militia ready). An appendage of the War Department, the civilian-run NBPRP had several trustees of the NRA on its executive board. This was a critical turning point for the NRA, because these trustees worked with Congress to pass Public Law 149, which authorized the sale of surplus military weapons, at cost, to rifle clubs meeting NBPRP standards. One of these standards was that the club had to be sponsored by the NRA.

In 1910, Congress authorized the giving away of surplus weaponry to NRA-sponsored clubs and in 1912 began funding NRA shooting matches. The association benefited greatly, and membership climbed from several hundred to several thousand by World War I. The end of World War I increased significantly the number of surplus weapons made available to the NRA, and membership rose steadily as prospective members were motivated by the allure of a free new rifle and a place to shoot it. By the mid-1930s, the first period in which the NRA actively involved itself in anti–gun control activity, the organization had grown to 35,000 members.[8]

The 1930s were ripe for gun control legislation. The nation had developed a serious gangster problem. Moreover, the traditional passivity of the federal government was being eroded because of the Great Depression, which forced the government to become involved in the health and welfare of the public to its greatest degree thus far. The various programs to counteract massive unemployment and poverty provided the foundation for a national effort to fight crime. While Franklin Roosevelt had been governor of New York, he strongly supported restrictive handgun licensing laws and the banning of machine guns; thus his election to the presidency further enhanced the prospects for federal gun control. He appointed Homer Cummings attorney general, head of the Justice Department. Cummings believed that the sale of machine guns should be highly regulated and that they should be registered. Moreover, he came to believe that *all* firearms should be registered. "Show me the man who does not want his gun registered and I will show you a man who should not have a gun" he proclaimed.[9] The bill that eventually became the National Firearms Act of 1934 was introduced in Congress with provisions to regulate the sale of machine guns *and,* much more importantly, to require that all handguns be registered. But the latter never came to pass.

Compared to what the organization would become in the 1980s, the NRA of the 1930s was moderate and restrained in its attempts to influence public policy. As characterized by two chroniclers of the era, "the NRA ... approach during the New Deal years was never wholly negativist."[10] In response to the proposed National Firearms Act, the NRA developed its first clear philosophy on gun control. Although recognizing the bill's virtuous aim of fighting gangsterism, the NRA deemed it a potential threat to firearms owners and decided to fight those portions of it that were not directly aimed at gangsters—namely the sections dealing with a system of national gun registration. This philosophy was revised and refined over the years until the late 1970s, when it was expanded and solidified to the point where it was deemed that virtually all gun control regulations should be resisted. The decision to oppose the gun registration portion of the 1934 bill was accompanied by the development of a strategy and set of tactics that have stayed with the NRA ever since. It circulated editorials, press releases, and open letters throughout the sporting and gun-owning communities. It urged its members and potential sympathizers to telegram or to write congressional representatives. The subsequent huge influx of antiregistration mail was instrumental in the deletion of reference to "all weaponry" and substitution of "machine guns and sawed-off shotguns" in the final version of the National Firearms Act.

The success of the NRA in minimizing the effect of the act led to its invitation to work with the Justice Department and Congress in developing the Federal Firearms Act of 1938. As with earlier legislation, the NRA accepted minimal regulation but made sure strong restrictions, such as a system of national licensing, were kept out of the law. The 1934 law imposed a tax on the interstate sale or transfer of machine guns, while the 1938 law established a mandatory licensing system for firearms manufacturers, importers, and dealers. However, pressure from the NRA caused Congress to delete what Attorney General Cummings and the Justice Department believed was the bill's most essential section, the power to prosecute shippers and manufacturers who put guns into the hands of fugitives or criminals convicted for crimes of violence. The NRA "protested that this structure would place an unfair burden on the commercial enterprises engaged in gun sales and transport. They offered modifying phrases that assured the act's debilitation; businesses would be liable to penalty only if they could be convicted of 'knowing or having reasonable cause to believe' that the purchaser had a criminal background."[11] This modified form of the law ensured that the prediction of then Assistant Attorney General Joseph Keenan would come true: "the government would be unable to obtain a conviction under that provision."[12]

Although the NRA was not especially large or well funded in the 1930s, it found its interests more or less readily accepted because there was no gun control movement and no organization dedicated to gun control (such as HCI) during the era. As the Leffs observe in "The Politics of Ineffectiveness: Federal Firearms Legislation, 1919–1938,"

the crux of the balance of power between [gun] regulators and antiregulators in the inter-war period [1920s/30s] was that the Justice Department fought its gun control crusade with less intense and less mobilized allies, while facing a committed and organized resistance. The consequence was that the nascent national gun lobby was in a strong position, not only to fight gun control, but to co-opt or redefine those initiatives that seemed likely to gain a following.... Using negotiations and communications skills to mobilize the attentive public on gun issues and to press their case with Congress, the gun lobby helped set the agenda for gun control. It was thus possible to neutralize both an activist Justice Department and the less intense and disorganized majority in the public who favored gun registration.

Contemporary scholars, perceiving a pattern of susceptibility in New Deal policy making to groups with defined interests and objectives, "would not find this outcome surprising or atypical."[13]

Thus, for the NRA, *political opportunity* (see figure 5.1) flourished. It was able to work a *political system* that was (and still is) amenable to pressure from a motivated interest group and to thereby achieve its own aims. Most importantly, it did not have to deal with a powerful *countermovement,* such as that which eventually developed in the 1980s and 1990s under the leadership of Handgun Control Incorporated. And it *exploited the communication technologies* of the era to activate its membership.

Until the creation of HCI and the rise of the modern gun movement, congressional interest in firearms regulations always followed on the heels of highly publicized gun violence—the gangsterism of the 1930s eventuated in the two firearms acts of that decade, while the 1968 Gun Control Act was a reaction to the assassinations and race-related gun violence of the 1960s. Lacking such high-profile episodes of gun savagery, the 1940s and 1950s lacked new federal attempts at gun control. However, this period saw a great strengthening in the NRA. After World War II, nine million demobilized veterans reentered civilian life with a new interest in firearms. Tens of thousands of ex-GIs joined the NRA, giving it a much greater potential to wield power over public policy. However, these new members had little interest in gun control issues *per se* and great interest in hunting. The NRA's programs and publications began to reflect this, and "gradually, almost imperceptibly, the [organization] changed from a quasi-governmental league devoted to military preparedness to a truly national group catering to the needs of all sportsmen carrying guns."[14] It is almost common knowledge today that the NRA's headquarters has affixed above its front doors "The Right of the People to Keep and Bear Arms, Shall Not Be Infringed" (the last half of the Second Amendment—recall from chapter 2 that the first half reads "A well regulated Militia, being necessary

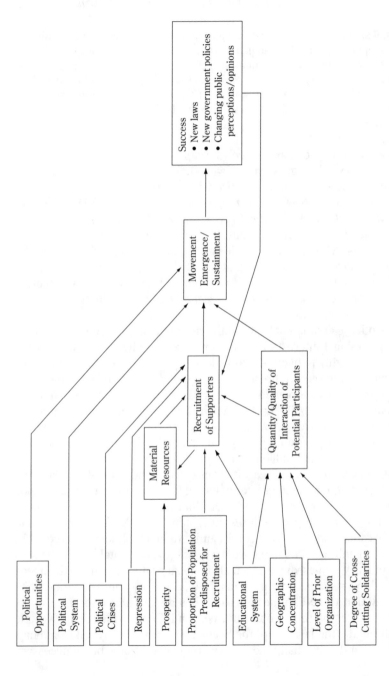

Figure 5.1. Social-Movement Theory: Macrolevel Constructs.

to the security of a free State"). However, in 1958, the NRA's main entrance was emblazoned with the words "Firearms Safety Education, Marksmanship Training, Shooting for Recreation."

Well into the 1970s, the NRA continued on a course that would seem quite moderate by today's standards. During congressional testimony over the proposed Gun Control Act of 1968, for example, NRA Executive Vice President Franklin Orth proclaimed "we do not think that any sane American, who calls himself an American, can object to placing into this bill the instrument which killed the president of the United States [John F. Kennedy]."[15] Equally as surprising, given its current inflexible position regarding gun regulation, the NRA of the late 1960s and early 1970s endorsed the banning of Saturday Night Specials (cheaply made handguns). In 1968, the NRA editorialized:

Shoddily manufactured by a few foreign makers, hundreds of thousands of these have been peddled in recent years by a handful of U.S. dealers. Prices as low as $8 or $10 have placed concealable handguns within reach of multitudes who never before could afford them. Most figure in "crimes of passion" or amateurish holdups, which form the bulk of the increase in violence. The Administration ... possesses sufficient authority to bar by Executive direction these miserably-made, potentially defective arms that contribute so much to rising violence.[16]

A highly favorable response from the membership followed this editorial, and the NRA reaffirmed its stance against Saturday Night Specials by observing that it did "not necessarily approve of everything that goes 'Bang!' "[17] Astoundingly (compared with the there-is-no-such-thing-as-a-good-gun-control-law position of the NRA today), Executive Vice President Orth even testified before Congress during its hearings on a proposed law that would ban Saturday Night Specials that "the National Rifle Association concurs in principle with the desirability of removing from the market crudely made and unsafe handguns ... [because] they have no sporting purpose, they are frequently poorly made.... On the Saturday Night Special, we are for [banning] it 100 percent. We would like to get rid of these guns."[18] However, the *we* Orth was speaking of was not the entire leadership of the NRA. Other parts of the organization, most notably its legislative and public-affairs division (which became the Institute for Legislative Action in 1975), were lobbying members of the House Judiciary Committee to pigeon-hole the Saturday Night Special bill—a lobbying effort that was ultimately successful, since this is where the proposed legislation eventually died.[19] As for the place of the Second Amendment in debate over gun control, the official *NRA Fact Book on Firearms Control* noted that it was of "limited practical utility" in arguing against gun control.[20]

The voices of moderation coming from the NRA changed in the late 1970s. Two factors were critical: the rise of the gun control movement and the 1977 palace coup by Second Amendment hard-liners who toppled a leadership that had heretofore seen the NRA as primarily a hunting and sport-shooting association.

Emergence of the Modern Gun Control Movement

The modern gun control movement began in 1974 when Mark Borinsky founded the National Council to Control Handguns (later renamed Handgun Control Incorporated). Borinsky had been robbed at gunpoint as a graduate student in Chicago. The experience was traumatic: One of the gunmen holding him up said at one point "let's shoot 'em." As Borinsky recalled later, "[w]hen you're young, you think you will live forever, that you're invulnerable. But that encounter robbed me of that feeling."[21] The trauma stayed with him, and upon graduation and moving to Washington, D.C., he decided to join a group promoting gun control to help prevent another young person from going through what he had experienced in Chicago. No such group existed, so he sought to fill the void by starting one.

To get his organization up and running, Borinsky enlisted the aid of recently retired CIA agent Edward Welles. Borinsky found Welles by advertising for others interested in the cause in a neighborhood newspaper, the *Northwest Current*. Welles did not have the bad-experience-with-guns motivation that many of HCI's early founders had but was motivated by a more general desire to "do something good for the community" in his retirement. Borinsky and Welles set up shop at 1710 H Street and soon had a telephone, a secretary, and a telephone directory with many influential Washington figures listed. The embryonic organization was given a huge boost in 1975 with the arrival of Pete Shields, whose 23-year-old son had been murdered with a handgun in San Francisco's 1974 Zebra Killings.[22] Shields had been directed to HCI by coworker Joe Clark, who happened to be a friend of Welles. Shields was a skilled marketing manager with many years of experience at E. I. du Pont de Nemours and Company. His organizational abilities, his natural suaveness in dealing with Washington's social and political moguls, and his quickly learned political savvy were critical for shaping HCI into the premier organization of the gun control movement.

Political opportunities (see figure 5.1) comprise the receptivity of the political system to social-movement activity.[23] Political opportunities are closely tied to the nature of the political system. Intuitively, one would expect receptivity to be higher in nations with democratic political systems compared to their totalitarian counterparts. However, within a nation, receptivity, whether out of the openness of the political system or out of some unexpected or undesired vulnerability, varies across time.

Political opportunities were ripe in the mid-1970s for the formation of HCI and the beginnings of the gun control movement. First, the era was close to the maelstroms of the 1960s, when social movements sprang up on an almost continuous basis. The 1960s zeitgeist encouraged individuals to view personal troubles as rooted in public issues and to see possible resolutions of these troubles by way of collective response—forming advocacy groups, building coalitions, engaging in pressure group politics (from demonstrating to lobbying). Although the 1970s were comparatively quiet on the social-movements front, the legacy of the 1960s was a continuation of a scaled-down version of its zeitgeist.[24] It is hard to imagine Borinsky and Welles having the same response to finding no gun control organization in 1954 as they had in 1974.

Second, the social movements of the 1960s were partly responsible for the enormous lobbying industry that had developed in Washington by the mid-1970s. The city had become a haven for interest groups wanting to influence government. When Borinsky and Welles decided to set up shop, the Washington phone book contained more than 2,500 listings that began with the words *National Association of* Formally registered lobbyists numbered in the thousands, and the number unregistered was even greater.[25] Moreover, in 1974, via its authorization of political action committees, Congress formalized ways—that were monitored and seemed ethical—for interest groups to give money to political candidates, which HCI quickly took advantage of. In short, Washington contained the culture, role models, motivations, and other mechanisms for starting a pressure group organization such as HCI.

Third, there was a real vacuum to fill in 1974. Although gun control had been among the interests of several groups—including the League of Women Voters, a variety of churches, and various governmental agencies (e.g., the U.S. Department of Justice)—from time to time during the twentieth century, there was no organization devoted specifically to the control of firearms. Had there been such an organization, odds are Borinsky and Welles would have joined it, and their talents and vision for what would become the gun control movement probably would not have been unleashed as energetically.

Finally, HCI found political opportunity within the federal government itself. Many members of Congress were sympathetic toward gun control and eager to work with an organization devoted to this issue. Indeed, many of these members had been part of the 78th Congress that had passed the first federal gun control legislation in 30 years—the 1968 Omnibus Crime Control & Safe Streets Act and the Federal Gun Control Act. These acts were in response to the assassinations and street violence of the 1960s; they banned mail-order purchase of firearms and regulated the interstate transportation and importation of guns and ammunition. However, the acts' banning of sales to felons, drug addicts, illegal aliens, and the mentally incompetent included no enforcement mechanism, and many members of Congress felt that rectifying this shortcoming was but one of many things yet to do regarding gun control. The Treasury Department's Bureau of Alcohol, Tobacco, and Firearms (BATF) welcomed an organization that would help in its fight to regulate and monitor firearms. BATF's efforts to fulfill the promise of the 1968 Gun Control Act had been stymied every step of the way by progun legislators (prodded, in part, by the NRA), and it needed any and every ally it could find. Most egregiously, BATF's proposal to begin a computerized system to record the serial numbers of all new weapons and to record every firearms transaction of the nation's 160,000 firearms licensees was slashed from its budget in committee.[26] Progun members of Congress had even made the battle personal, as seen, for example, in Michigan Representative John Dingell's accusation that BATF's investigators were "jackbooted fascists."[27]

The Department of Justice also welcomed an organization devoted to gun control. The department's recently formed Bureau of Justice Statistics contained many staffers who were shocked by the gun violence statistics they were amassing and subsequently eager to provide these statistics in editorialized format ("guns are bad, just look at these data!") to the newly formed HCI. In later years, HCI found an ally in the federal government's Centers for Disease Control, whose staffers were affected by the gun violence data they were analyzing in much the same way as their counterparts in the Bureau of Justice Statistics.[28]

The *level of prior organization* has immediate and direct influence on a social movement's prospects for success. The most prominent example in recent American history was the role of African-American churches and colleges as collective settings in which the organizing work of the civil rights movement took place.[29] The founders of Handgun Control Incorporated also benefited—at least to a small degree—from prior organization. At about the same time HCI was being formed, the Board of Church and Society of the Methodist Church established the National Coalition to Ban Handguns (NCBH). This coalition brought together 30 religious, labor, and nonprofit organizations to develop a plan for combating violence in America by getting handguns banned. Their role models were countries such as Japan and the Netherlands, which had handgun bans and almost nonexistent gun violence.

HCI, then still calling itself the National Coalition to Control Handguns, became a member of NCBH and profited from its interactions with groups that had lobbying and organizing experience. It was within the context of NCBH that HCI's founders refined and clarified their ideology and initial strategies to combat gun violence. Borinsky and Shields were able to fully reconceptualize their individual tragedies (Borinsky having been robbed at gunpoint and Shields losing his son to gunfire) as a public issue (widespread gun violence as a result of the unchecked spread of handguns throughout American society), an issue that demanded a public resolution (strict controls on handguns and other firearms). To paraphrase Jeanne Shields, the widow of Pete Shields, he was able to see that his pain was felt by many, as well as the possibility of easing this pain through what grew into HCI.[30] In short, within the confines of a small but critically important group, there occurred a *collective attribution that a social problem existed* and a collective sense of what needed to be done to correct it. In the simplest possible terms, this framing of the problem—this collective attribution, this ideology that the gun control movement now promulgates—became "guns destroy, guns must be controlled."

However, when HCI changed its goal from the outright banning to the strict control of handguns, it withdrew from NCBH. The decision to change goals was based on political reality. Public-opinion polls were consistently showing (and still do show—see figure 4.2) that the American population was not ready for a Japanese- or European-style ban on handguns but was willing to accept strict regulations such as licensing, registration, and waiting periods. Moreover, several congressional supporters of gun control emphasized to HCI's leaders that any attempt to put an outright ban on handguns was "a position that is unwinnable because it is politically unrealistic."[31] Thus, HCI's position in 1976 of making "the possession of *all* handguns and *all* handgun ammunition ... totally illegal" was transmuted into seeking strict controls but still allowing "the right of law-abiding citizens to possess handguns for legitimate purposes."[32]

HCI also profited from its associations with the Washington law firms Covington-Burling-Wilmer and Cutler-Pickering. Both firms devote significant time to *pro bono publico* work, and both firms saw the budding gun control group as a worthy project. They provided their experience and expertise in helping HCI become a legal, corporate entity and assisted its founders in developing legislative strategies.[33]

Although far from a powerful force in Washington during this decade, by the mid-1970s, HCI was well on its way to learning the ins and outs of Capitol Hill, and its president, Pete Shields, was becoming a familiar face at congressional committee hearings on the issue of gun control. More importantly, the founders of HCI were learning rule number one for successful lobbying: You have to *look* like somebody before you can *be* somebody. Or, in the words of longtime Washington correspondent Robert Sherrill, "reputation is half a lobby's strength."[34] So they set out to give the appearance of having clout in the hopes of someday realizing it.

When *People* magazine and the *New Yorker* did small write-ups on HCI, the organization had the articles reproduced and distributed by the thousands. Although it had only a few thousand dues-paying members, HCI wanted to make its roster as impressive as possible. It actively recruited political, sports, and entertainment-industry celebrities, and when support was received from two dozen of them, HCI quickly put their names on the letterhead used for mass mailings. Celebrity names included Steve Allen, Arthur Ashe, Leonard Bernstein, Ellen Burstyn, Julia Child, Hal Holbrook, Maynard Jackson, Martin Luther King Sr., Ann Landers, John Lindsay, Milton Eisenhower, Richard Hatcher, Marsha Mason, William Ruckelshaus, Neil Simon, and Roy Wilkens.

This air of power and respectability bred success. In early 1976, HCI cultivated close ties with several members of the House Judiciary

Committee, and it appeared the committee would vote 18–14 to recommend passage of a bill that would prohibit the manufacture of Saturday Night Specials. During the preceding two years, HCI had been charming the halls of Capitol Hill without ever seeing the NRA. But now, with what appeared like the imminent passage of the first congressional gun control legislation since the Gun Control Act of 1968—legislation that was truly being helped along by HCI—the NRA roared into action. The weekend before the final Judiciary Committee vote, Harlon Carter, NRA's executive director, sent the following Mailgram to the NRA's membership in the congressional districts represented on the Judiciary Committee:

Dear NRA Member:

The House Judiciary Committee is moving quickly toward final approval of HR 11193 the Federal Firearms Act of 1976. Contrary to what the media has reported HR 11193 is one of the strongest anti-gun bills ever to be considered by the Congress. The bill would outlaw three-quarters of all handguns now manufactured or imported and ban the sale or inheritance of millions already in private hands. The bill's restrictions on dealers also will severely limit availability of long guns as well as ammunition. The Judiciary Committee meets again Thursday, February 26, 1976. Your Congressman, the Honorable _____, Phone _____ is on the committee. Please telephone or wire him immediately and urge him to vote against HR 11193. Also get your friends to contact him to vote against HR 11193.

Harlon B. Carter
Executive Director

Even though the Mailgram was misleading—Judiciary Committee member Martin Russo (Democrat, Illinois) called a press conference to explain that there were no provisions to "severely limit availability of long guns as well as ammunition"—it fulfilled its aim: Key members of the Judiciary Committee received a flood of Mailgrams and telephone calls. By February 26, four members changed their votes (Illinois Republican Thomas Railsback, California Democrat George Danielson, Illinois Republican Henry Hyde, and New York Democrat Edward Patterson). Danielson reported getting 300 Mailgrams and phone calls from NRA members, while Patterson told HCI's Pete Shields he had received 400.[35] Clearly, just as described in the theoretical literature on social movements, HCI and the fledgling gun control movement had produced a countermovement led by the NRA.

The NRA-Led Countermovement

The key difference between the two movements was the far stronger *original organizing group* of the anti–gun control movement, the NRA. Given the size and reputation of the NRA, what became critical to the launching of the countermovement was the "frame *re*alignment" that a radically conservative faction of the NRA's leadership orchestrated in the mid-1970s: getting the membership to collectively believe that there was a new social problem arising in America—one that was tantamount to a national crisis—gun control legislation. This new mental schema viewed all gun regulation as "bad." Furthermore, the schema held out a new primary role for the NRA: What had heretofore been mainly a sportsman's association was now to have as its major purpose opposing the gun control movement. Although some of the NRA's membership and leadership had always been radically opposed to any form of gun regulation, they were in the minority. In 1972, however, this minority began an all-out—and eventually successful—effort to redefine the meaning and the mission of the NRA.

Executive committee member Harlon B. Carter led this redefinition effort. In a July 1972 address to the NRA executive committee, Carter argued that the previous NRA philosophy on gun control—that some was necessary and good for society—was wrongheaded and needed to be replaced by a new philosophy, one of absolute resistance to any and all forms of gun regulation: "Any position we took [on gun control] back at that time is no good, it is not valid, and it is simply not relevant to the problem that we face today. The latest news release from NRA embraces a disastrous concept ... that evil is imputed to the sale and delivery, the possession of a certain kind of firearm, entirely apart from the good or evil intent of the man who uses it and/or ... that the legitimate use of a handgun is limited to sporting use."[36]

Carter argued further that every gun had a legitimate purpose and that every law-abiding person, no matter what his or her age, should have the right to choose his or her own weapon according to what he or she thought best. The argument was even carried to the point that children, because of their tiny hands, should have access to derringers: "There was a little boy ... and it was real cold and he had his hands in his overcoat. He had one of these little old derringers, and four bushy guys ambled up in an arrogant manner. He stopped them, and three of them were very nice and decent, and one of them said, 'What would you do if I told you I had a pistol and I was going to kill you?' And he said, 'I would kill you, you son-of-a-bunch.' These little guns have a very noble and a very important place and we should make our position clear."[37] What about Saturday Night Specials? Carter argued that "good guys" would never own them, and that when "bad guys" went to use them, sometimes the guns misfired and this "has saved many, many lives, and the question arises: What are we trying to do? Upgrade the quality of handguns in the hands of our criminals?"

Largely through Carter's efforts, the minority view began appearing more and more in the NRA's public statements. The moderate editorials that had sometimes appeared in the NRA's *American Rifleman* disappeared as its editor during the 1960s was replaced, partly through pressure applied by Carter, by a former *Saturday Evening Post* editor "who would really raise hell with anyone who even suggested there could be anything good about any kind of gun control."[38] Moreover, Carter shielded him from criticism, and the new editor was able to run the *American Rifleman* "virtually independent of any control" from moderate members on the executive committee, including the president, F. M. Hakenjos.[39] The redefinition of the NRA culminated in the revolt at Cincinnati in 1977. During the mid-1970s, only 25 percent of the organization—according to the NRA's own estimate—consisted of "nonshooting constitutionalists" (people dedicated to preserving full-scale private ownership of firearms).[40] But this did not prevent the complete takeover of NRA leadership positions by the hardest of the hard-liners against gun control at the NRA's 1977 annual meeting.

The coup was led by Carter (who had recently resigned from the newly formed lobbying arm of the NRA, the Institute for Legislative Action, to show his disgust at the moderate leadership and the directions it was taking the organization), Neal Knox (editor of the gun magazines *Rifle* and *Handloader*), Robert Kukla (the new head of the Institute for Legislative Action), and Joseph Tartaro (the editor of *Gun Week*). In late 1976, these four and others banded together to form an ad hoc committee they called the Federation for NRA. Many members of the committee had been fired by moderate executives in November 1976 in what had been dubbed the "weekend massacre." Although the firings had been justified as a cost-saving and streamlining measure, only Second Amendment hard-liners had been let go. The Federation viewed the NRA's willingness to compromise on gun control as anathema.

The new political agenda was also unacceptable to the Federation. Moderate leaders such as Maxwell Rich and Franklin Orth saw the future of NRA's political activity in the area of environmental law; the NRA would join the Sierra Club, Greenpeace, and other conservation organizations in working for legislation to protect wilderness areas from mining and ranching interests and from uncontrolled public access. Symbolic of this new agenda was the changing of the name of a 37,000-acre tract of land newly acquired by the NRA in New Mexico from the National *Shooting* Center to the National *Outdoor* Center. Also symbolic was a plan to move the NRA's headquarters from Washington, D.C., to Colorado Springs (not far from the Outdoor Center). "That might make the task of lobbying Congress more difficult, but then legislative action was no longer an NRA priority."[41]

Using their years of experience in organizing and taking full advantage of their networks of allies in the NRA membership, the leaders of the Federation planned their revolt carefully and effectively. They began by using their access to gun publications to excoriate the directions the NRA was taking and to defame those on the executive committee who were in support of these directions. Next, at the convention itself, they used their knowledge of parliamentary procedure—as well as walkie-talkies on the convention floor to move their supporters around to various committee meetings—to methodically replace top leaders with members from the Federation and to radically alter the course the NRA had been taking toward being a hunting and conservation organization. The new NRA would become the gun lobby. In the words of Carter, "[b]eginning at this place and at this hour, this period in NRA is finished."

The "New NRA" (as Carter now called it) sought to give itself more clout on Capitol Hill by bulking up its membership. A growing membership would be critical not only for bolstering the budget and giving an appearance that the organization represented a significant portion of Americana, but also to enhance the NRA's chief tactic for influencing Congress: using members to put direct pressure on legislators. More specifically, the NRA began contacting its members with "legislative alerts," asking them to communicate directly with their legislators to request that gun control legislation be quashed.

To recruit new members, the NRA relied heavily on *selective incentives.* Prospective members were—and are still being—lured into the organization by a low membership fee ($15 in the late 1970s; up to $35 in the mid-1990s) that would yield many returns: a year's subscription to the *American Rifleman* or the *American Hunter;* low-cost gun liability, theft, accidental death, dismemberment, cancer, and hospitalization insurance; a discount on moving household goods via North American Van Lines; and an inexpensive major credit card.

To encourage members to recruit their friends and relatives, the NRA offered "get-a-member" and "enlist-a-friend" giveaways such as belt buckles, hats, key chains, patches, and coffee mugs. In its recruiting drives, the NRA used advertisements that implanted or magnified the fear in hunters and sport shooters that the real aim of HCI and the gun control movement was the total banning of all firearms; this would not only spoil the sport for gun owners and prevent them from defending themselves in a crime-ridden society but also violate the fundamental constitutional right of all Americans to keep and bear arms. Thus, new members clearly understood that the New NRA was going to be a highly political organization; indeed, by the mid-1990s, a *Time* magazine poll found 93 percent of them "totally satisfied" with the new, no-compromise leadership.[42]

The membership drive was nearly a complete success. Although many old-timers left the organization, they were replaced many times over by newcomers who were much more in tune with the NRA's new agenda of being *the* gun lobby. Before the Cincinnati Revolt, membership was a little more than a million; by 1983, it had swelled to 2.6 million, and it continued to grow into the early 1990s when it peaked at 3.6 million. Although the new membership is more politically in tune with objectives of the New NRA, selective incentives are still critical: In 1989, when annual membership dues were raised from $20 to $25, the organization lost 15 percent of its members. Again, in 1995, when dues were raised from $25 to $35, a significant decline in membership occurred; however, some of this 8 percent decline was also likely in response to the NRA's stance against the Brady Handgun Control Act and the assault-weapons ban contained in the 1994 Violent Crime Control and Law Enforcement Act. As of early 1996, membership was holding steady at about 3.2 million.[43]

The New NRA was bolstered by the 1980 presidential election of lifetime member and arch conservative Ronald Reagan. Indeed, Reagan was the first president ever to attend an NRA annual convention, where in 1983 he mounted the podium with Harlon Carter and proclaimed to roaring applause: "You live by Lincoln's words, 'Important principles may and must be inflexible.' . . . the Constitution does not say government shall *decree* the right to keep and bear arms. The Constitution says 'the right of the people to keep and bear arms shall not be infringed.' "[44] Reagan made a promise on the podium to support the NRA's agenda: He would work on behalf of NRA-backed legislation and stand shoulder to shoulder with it in opposing antigun legislation: "[W]e will never disarm any American who seeks to protect his or her family from fear or harm."[45]

NRA power was at its peak. Its Institute for Legislative Action grew to a staff of 50, including seven full-time lobbyists. Its Political Victory Fund (founded in 1975) was channeling millions of dollars into state and national elections in support of candidates that were rated "A" on its gun control scorecard. The crowning achievement of the era was passage, under the guidance of a conservative Republican president and Senate, of the Firearm Owners' Protection Act of 1986, legislation that the NRA had lobbied hard for. This act abrogated many of the regulations contained in the 1968 Gun Control Act, most notably reinstating the interstate sale of rifles and shotguns and abolishing record-keeping requirements for ammunition dealers.

Politics and Gun Control

Between 1968 and 1988, no gun control measure left committee to be voted on by either floor of Congress (the 1986 Firearm Owners' Protection Act was *anti*–gun control). In the late 1970s, HCI and its allies were too small and too inexperienced to have much impact on the legislative process, and they were in no way ready to do serious battle with the progun lobby lead by the NRA. Even though President Jimmy Carter was an advocate of strong gun control, he could find no outside ally to battle the influence of the NRA on Capitol Hill and in the media, and he feared the political consequences of fighting what he was convinced would be a losing battle[46] However, by the early 1980s, HCI had grown to 80,000 members and had an operating budget in the millions of dollars. Although it would take almost another decade for it to win any significant battles and get national gun control legislation passed, HCI began fighting the progun lobby in Washington and in state and local legislatures as it started courting the press.

Political crises often encourage the formation of new social movements and the invigoration of older ones. Unpopular wars, hyperinflation, assassinations, and similar calamities have encouraged great and small revolutions alike.[47] This phenomenon has indirect applicability to the gun control movement. John Hinckley's use of a cheap handgun in March of 1981 to shoot President Ronald Reagan and his press secretary, James Brady, eventuated in a boon for HCI and the gun control movement. The assassination attempt generated huge media focus on handguns, their all-too-easy acquisition, and their all-too-strong connection with violence, thereby promulgating and giving credibility to HCI's number-one argument that the United States was in need of more controls on its firearms.

The assassination attempt also motivated Sarah Brady, James Brady's wife, to dedicate herself to the gun control movement; she joined HCI and ultimately became its president. Finally, the assassination attempt prompted Congress to take up the issue of gun control again, and legislation was introduced that eventually became the 1988 Undetectable Firearms Act (banning the manufacture, importation, possession, receipt, and transfer of plastic guns, which can evade metal detectors) and the 1993 Brady Handgun Violence Prevention Act (which requires a five-day waiting period and a criminal background check before an individual can purchase a handgun; more on this law later). Relatedly, the assassination attempt was in the mind of Congress when, at the urging of HCI, it banned the interstate sale of pistols as part of the 1986 Firearms Owners' Protection Act, an act that was otherwise anti–gun control in its dismantling of many provisions of the 1968 Gun Control Act.

The murder of John Lennon in December of 1980—also carried out with a cheap pistol—likewise greatly heightened public and media interest in and sympathy for the kind of strict national control of guns that HCI was promoting. Lennon's assassination took the organization from 5,000 to 80,000 dues-paying members in a matter of weeks.

Political opportunities for HCI and the gun control movement expanded unexpectedly in 1988. The Republican platform for the 1988 election of George Bush had included support for the "constitutional right to keep and bear arms." Bush himself was a card-carrying member of the NRA and generally considered to be progun. However, Patrick Purdy's January 1989 massacre of children at a Stockton, California, school yard—in which he killed 5 and wounded 29 others—motivated a change of heart in President Bush. Purdy used an AK-47 assault rifle, imported from China, to rapidly fire 105 rounds.[48] By executive order, Bush quickly announced a temporary ban on the importation of AK-47s and selected similar rifles.[49] This sparked the introduction of several bills in Congress to outlaw or restrict assault pistols and rifles. However, it took the election of a Democratic president, Bill Clinton, in 1992 to finally broker one of these bills through Congress. Clinton used every political medium at a president's disposal to pressure Congress to include one of these bills as part of the 1994 Violent Crime Control and Law Enforcement Act, which banned 19 different types of assault weapons.[50]

Political opportunity reached its peak for the gun control movement during the 1992–1994 period. The Democratic platform on which Clinton was elected contained strong gun control language. It aimed to "shut down the weapons bazaars" and the gun black market; require a waiting period for handgun purchases; ban assault weapons; and enact severe punishments for those selling guns to children or using guns in the commission of crime. Since 1987, the top priority of HCI had been passage of the Brady bill (named in honor of White House Press Secretary James Brady, who had been seriously wounded during John Hinckley's 1981 attempt to assassinate President Reagan). The bill required a week-long waiting period for those purchasing handguns. The waiting period provided a cooling-off interval for those wanting to buy handguns during fits of rage and also allowed police to do a background check on prospective buyers to ensure their mental competence and lack of criminal past.

The bill was defeated in the House of Representatives in September 1988, in part because of a multimillion-dollar effort by the NRA.[51] A version of the bill was passed by both houses of Congress in spring 1991; however, the House–Senate compromise bill was killed by Republican filibuster twice during 1992. Presidential power can overcome this kind of problem, and George Bush could have done so if he had found the commitment that Bill Clinton had the following year. Indeed, former NRA chief lobbyist Wayne LaPierre would later characterize Clinton's 1993 efforts as "the most intensive lobbying and arm-twisting effort ever conducted by a president of the United States on a gun control bill."[52] The bill was enacted in November, with two key compromises to avoid another Senate filibuster. First, the week-long waiting period was reduced to five business days, and second, police would be required to do background checks only for five years, after which an "instant-check" computerized system would be used (the bill provided $200 million per year to help the states upgrade their computerized records so they could be used in an instant-check system).

Passage of the Brady bill opened up more political opportunity for the gun control movement, demonstrating that the heretofore perceived omnipotence of the NRA was exaggerated. As summarized by New York House Democrat and gun control proponent Charles E. Schumer, members of Congress "realized that there's life after voting against the NRA."[53] Gun control proponents were quick to press their advantage, and the assault-weapons-ban portion of the 1994 Violent Crime Control and Law Enforcement Act represented one of their finest moments.

Glowing with success, HCI worked with its congressional allies Senator Howard M. Metzenbaum and Representative Charles E. Schumer to quickly put together what HCI proudly deemed Brady II. Formally entitled the Handgun Control and Violence Protection Act of 1994, this bill sought to establish a national licensing requirement for handgun possession; prohibit multiple handgun purchases or transfers (no more than one per 30-day period would be allowable); mandate that all handgun dealers be strictly licensed; require that all guns be registered with BATF; set up measures to ensure that all gun dealers be of the legitimate storefront type, requiring a heavy licensing fee ($1,000; historically the fee was a paltry $60 but increased to $200 by the Brady Handgun Control Act); establish tort liability for firearms dealers; require that the treasury secretary set up security precautions to be taken by firearms dealers; prohibit the sale or transfer of firearms to convicted violent felons or persons under court order; require a special federal license for ammunition dealers; redefine and regulate the use of "armor-piercing ammunition"; and, finally, provide mandatory minimum penalties for gunrunning, firearms and explosives thefts, use of semiautomatic firearms by criminals, use of firearms in drug trafficking, and possession of a gun by convicted violent felons or serious drug offenders.[54] Brady II was the gun control movement's *pièce de résistance*. Its passage would put the regulation of firearms in the United States on par with that in many other industrialized democracies. It would be a crowning achievement of gun control proponents in the 104th Congress (1995–1996).

However, the congressional elections of November 8, 1994, quickly diminished political opportunity for the gun control movement. Although gun control *per se* was not a hot issue during the campaign season, the NRA spent several million dollars campaigning actively against what it had rated its "F" candidates, concentrating its appeals on concerns other than gun control (e.g., on an incumbent's not keeping election promises and on "family values"; with 90 percent of the electorate in support of the Brady Handgun Control Law, the NRA wisely decided that direct progun appeals would be inopportune).[55] The gun control side of Congress suffered devastating defeats. Many prominent and powerful members lost their seats—among them House Speaker Thomas S. Foley (Democrat, Washington), House Judiciary Chair Jack Brooks (Democrat, Texas), and Senate Budget Committee Chair Jim Sasser (Democrat, Tennessee, who was also a contender for majority leader). And many up-and-comers who had advocated gun control were also swept aside, including House members Thomas Andrews (Democrat, Maine), James Cooper (Democrat, Tennessee), Sam Coppersmith (Democrat, Arizona), "Buddy" Darden (Democrat, Georgia), Jay Inslee (Democrat, Washington), Don Johnson (Democrat, Georgia), Michael Kreidler (Democrat, Georgia), and Richard Swett (Democrat, New Hampshire). In sum, conservative Republican candidates, many of them rated "A" on NRA's scorecard of legislators, were elected in enough states and congressional districts for Republicans to gain control of both houses of Congress. Eighty percent of NRA-endorsed candidates won their elections, including 41 conservative Democrats. In the House of Representatives, "47 anti-gunners, 22 wafflers, and 16 solid pro-gunners were replaced by 70 NRA-rated 'A's,' seven 'B's' or unknowns, and eight 'F's.' "[56]

Understanding the American political system is critical to grasping the sustainment and varying success of the gun control movement. A Democratic Congress in both houses and a Democrat president were essential to the success of HCI and the gun control movement during the early 1990s, the only period in which the movement has achieved significant national legislative success (which is its primary goal). Republican control of the Senate between 1980 and 1986 and after the 1994 elections and of the House of Representatives since 1994 essentially halted gun control legislation. Indeed, House Majority Leader Newt Gingrich publicly avowed that "no gun-control legislation is going to move in committee or on the floor of this House" as long as Republicans held sway.[57]

As revealed in chapter 4, political conservatism and support for control are inversely related. More importantly, the majority party appoints chairs of congressional committees, and this fact alone almost assures that Gingrich can live up to his promise. Nearly all proposed legislation begins and dies (95 percent) in committees. Committee chairs have considerable power. They decide when a bill will come up for discussion, how long the discussion will be, and whether staff hired to assist the committee will work on this bill or another.[58]

Not only did the new Republican House Majority Leader Newt Gingrich aver that "no gun-control legislation is going to move" during his tenure, but he took further action in creating the Second Amendment Legislative Task Force "to develop a comprehensive strategy and plan that will *restore* rights of our citizenry to keep and bear arms, in accordance with the Second Amendment of the Constitution."[59] The task force's first action was to develop H.R. 1488, a bill to repeal the 1994 assault-weapons ban. To add insult to injury, on November 8, 1994, the U.S. Supreme Court struck down the 1990 Gun-Free School Zones Act, which had prohibited the possession of firearms within 1,000 feet of any school; the Court concurred with a 1993 Fifth Circuit Court ruling that the authority Congress used to justify the law—their control over interstate commerce—was misused.[60] Finally, during the same period, federal judges in Arizona, Louisiana, Montana, and New Mexico were striking down portions of the Brady law, ruling that the federal government had exceeded its authority in mandating that local police do the required background checks.[61]

Political opportunities can change quickly, literally overnight (as they did on November 8, 1994). The era of the 104th Congress was shaping up to be a bleak time for the gun control movement. Although more than two dozen gun control bills had been introduced in the new Congress,[62] it appeared the fate of all of them—including HCI's flagship legislation, H.R. 1321/S. 631 (Brady II)—was to languish in congressional committees, never reaching a vote on either the House or the Senate floor. However, the winds of fortune took an abrupt turn on April 19, 1995, when two gun-toting militia members, Timothy McVeigh and Terry Nichols, were implicated in the bombing of the Alfred P. Murrah Federal Building in Oklahoma City that took 167 lives. Media reports emphasized the connection between the militias and the free-and-easy wide-open market for obtaining military-type weapons in the United States.[63] Several gun control advocates in Congress (most notably Charles Schumer) also emphasized the same connection.[64] Public opinion toward militia groups soured,[65] and almost immediately, antiterrorist bills were introduced in both houses of Congress.

House Judiciary Chairman Henry Hyde—a Republican from Illinois who campaigned in the 1980s on a progun platform but had a change of heart in the 1990s and became a staunch proponent of the Brady bill—sponsored H.R. 1710, a bill containing many gun-related provisions that were in step with the gun control movement's agenda for national-level gun laws; indeed, HCI lobbied heavily for it. The antiterrorist act proposed a mandatory prison sentence on anyone transferring a firearm that there was reasonable cause to believe would be used in a violent crime. This seemed like a sensible regulation to the proponents of gun control. But to some on the progun side, such a regulation was unthinkable: "This is a loaded gun pointed at the head of the American firearms industry.... [A] manufacturer/seller could be prosecuted under the reasoning that 'Out of all the guns you sold, you should have known that some would wind up in the wrong hands.' This provision could conceivably drive gun manufacturers and gun dealers out of business."[66]

H.R. 1710 defines *terrorism* as the use of an explosive or firearm "other than for mere personal monetary gain [i.e., robbery], with intent to endanger, directly or indirectly, the safety of one or more individuals or to cause substantial property damage." This definition was again intolerable for many progun activists: "It elevates many current state crimes to the federal level. 'Every crime in the country involving carrying a gun or explosive—other than simple robbery—now becomes a federal offense, and not only that, a terrorist act.' This means brandishing a firearm to discourage criminal activity could suddenly become a federal offense, subjecting a person to oftentimes less-than-sympathetic federal prosecutors and mandatory prison terms."[67] Despite such outcries, reflected in the lobbying efforts of the NRA and its allies, the Antiterrorism and Effective Death Penalty Act eventually passed both houses of Congress in the spring of 1996.[68]

Gun control proponents lost the modicum of momentum they had gained with the Oklahoma bombing incident and the subsequent antiterrorist legislation when congressional battles with President Clinton over the budget essentially shut down the government in fall and early winter of 1995–1996. Almost all the legislation passed during this period consisted of temporary budget bills aimed at keeping various branches of the government open for time spans ranging from a few weeks to several months.

The 1996 election heavily influenced the political opportunity of the gun control movement through the year 2000. Clinton's reelection makes repeal of the Brady law or of the assault-weapons ban doubtful because he has pledged to veto any legislation directed against them. And as even many of the most ardent gun control opponents admit, the makeup of the current Congress will not allow for the override of a presidential veto of any progun legislation during the 105th Congress.[69]

Other Aspects of the Movement

The potential for HCI to grow is enormous (see proportion of population predisposed for recruitment, figure 5.1). As shown in table 4.1, support for gun control legislation is extremely high in all demographic groups except for hunters (and even then, the majority of hunters, 53 percent, supports gun control). Because hunters comprise no more than 15 to 20 percent of the adult population,[70] potentially 150 to 160 million individuals over the age 18 could be targeted for HCI membership and participation in the gun control movement.[71] Of course, only a tiny fraction of the population ever offers active support to any social movement; but percentages as high as 4 and 5 are not unknown, which would still leave a realizable potential of six to seven million members.[72]

The *educational system* of a society can influence social-movement activity in several ways; most importantly, movements are encouraged where there are many colleges and universities. The United States has 3,688 institutions of higher education,[73] and about half of the adult population has had at least one year of college attendance.[74] The college atmosphere stimulates movement activity by bringing together large numbers of individuals, many of whom are like-minded and have considerable free time. Colleges also produce many individuals who enter the labor market with high personal expectations for themselves and progressive values for society, which makes them ripe for recruitment into social movements promising a better lifestyle for themselves and for society in general. These facts are not lost on HCI, and it has recently begun an active campaign to do grassroots recruiting on college campuses and even in high schools.[75] These heretofore untapped resources can only bolster the gun control movement in coming years.

Post–World War II *prosperity* has helped the gun control movement, as it has done for all social movements since the 1960s. Hiring full-time lobbyists, full-time researchers, and full-time grassroots organizers is expensive, as is the operation and maintenance of full-time offices in the East (Washington, D.C.), the Midwest (Chicago), and the West (Los Angeles, San Diego, and San Francisco). On its membership application, HCI provides checkoff boxes of $15, $35, or $100—but letters accompanying applications sometimes ask for an additional "special contribution of $50, $75, or even $100 as your share in helping" the cause of gun control[76]; because HCI lobbies Congress, contributions to it are not tax deductible, even though it is a nonprofit organization (note, though, that contributions to HCI's sister organization, the Center to Prevent Handgun Violence, are tax deductible). Thus, one would expect its membership to be heavily middle class or above. Although HCI does not collect demographic background data on its membership, we would expect the bias toward the middle class to yield a high proportion of college-educated individuals. Indeed, as shown in table 4.1, individuals with bachelor and graduate degrees are more likely to support gun control legislation, which is not atypical of the newer social movements (animal rights, antihunger, antinuclear, women's rights, gay rights, ecology/environmental).[77] The ability of the estimated 400,000 dues-paying members[78] to support HCI's seven-million-dollar budget and CPHV's four-million-dollar budget greatly enhanced its power in the early 1990s. During the heyday of the NRA's power in the early to mid-1980s, HCI membership was estimated to be less than 100,000.[79]

The *degree of cross-cutting solidarities* refers to how well various groups in a society are integrated and the number and quality of linkages among them. In general, cross-cutting solidarities and social-movement emergence or support are inversely related. An ongoing problem with the women's movement, for example, is that most women live with men, which makes it hard for them to think of men as enemies and makes it easy for them to rationalize the desirability of men and women enacting complementary roles (he worries about money, she worries about home). As observed by Anthony Oberschall, one force behind the emergence of the civil rights movement was lack of cross-cutting solidarities between blacks and whites. African Americans were both socially and residentially segregated, which allowed for indigenous leaders to arise and for the creation of an us (blacks—discriminated against/suffering) versus them (whites—privileged/non-suffering) mind-set.[80] Similarly, the most vehement wing of the antiabortion movement draws its supporters from individuals who are "*encapsulated,* having no significant social ties to groups outside those which would reinforce their worldview."[81]

The cross-cutting solidarities factor is relevant to the gun control movement. As demonstrated in chapter 4, nonhunting, non–gun-owning individuals living in urbanized areas are the most likely to be supportive of the goals of the gun control movement, while gun-owning, rural hunters are the least likely. These two subpopulations of American society have distinctive subcultures and limited social ties.

Region by region, the correlation between "hunters per 1,000 population" and "percentage of the population favoring gun control" is inverse and moderately strong. For example, in New England there are 63 hunters per 1,000 people and more than 90 percent of the adult population favors gun control, whereas in the Mountain states the equivalent figures are 190 hunters and 75 percent.[82] Congressional support for the Brady Handgun Control Act of 1993, the crowning moment thus far of the gun control movement, varied dramatically by region. The act passed 238–189 in the House and 63–36 in the Senate (had the voting followed public opinion, with 87 percent of the adult population then in support of the Brady bill, the votes would have been 378–57 in the House and 87–13 in the Senate). Lowest support came from the rural districts and states. For example, in the House, 82 percent of Northern Democrats voted for the bill, while 55 percent of Southern Democrats gave their support. "As has been true with other gun bill votes, the strongest opposition came from southern, western, and rural representatives (rural districts are concentrated in the South and West), regardless of party. Strongest support came from urban representatives."[83]

Although HCI seeks broad support of its organization and its goals, it concentrates its recruitment in liberal, urban areas—as manifested, for example, by the locations of its regional offices (Chicago, Los Angeles, San Diego, San Francisco, and Washington, D.C.). In 1995, HCI organized 29 summit meetings to recruit and organize activists. Every such meeting was in a major urban area.[84] In contrast, the NRA finds its greatest support from gun-owning middle-class conservatives[85] and from hunters who possess multiple firearms, including at least one handgun.[86] HCI admits that in "small towns and rural communities ... the NRA goes unchallenged."[87]

Considering potential participation from a microlevel (individual) perspective (see figure 5.2), we may note that *prior contact with a movement supporter* is the single most important factor predicting involvement in a social-movement organization.[88] Having a friend, relative, coworker, or fellow student who is already involved in a social movement encourages one to become a movement supporter; the movement member can supply information, use his or her emotional attachment with the prospective recruit as a resource in motivating a

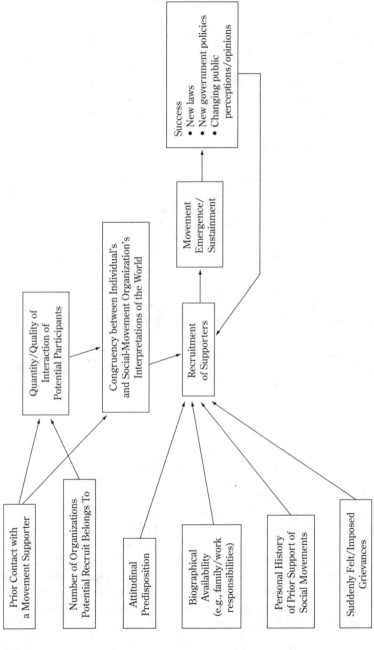

Figure 5.2. Social-Movement Theory: Microlevel Constructs

deeper examination of the movement, and, most importantly, facilitate the potential recruit to begin interpreting reality in accordance with movement ideology.[89] HCI relies heavily on personal contacts to recruit supporters at its grassroots local-level chapters in some three dozen cities. Indeed, this is how the organization obtained some of its initial funding: Pete Shields, Edward Welles, and a few other early founders of HCI used their Christmas card lists to seek donations. Shields described the response they got as "very good," especially "considering the non-professionalism of our approach."[90]

A more recent example of how the process works at its maximal level is found in the recruiting activities of Dr. William Gonda, a pediatrician in San Francisco. He spreads the HCI word to all of his patients' parents, counseling them "about the dangers of gun violence in the home" and getting them to begin "thinking about whether there are guns accessible in the homes their young children visit." He emphasizes that this is a "very political issue" that requires collective vigilance and action. Dr. Gonda also regularly distributes HCI information packets on how to stop firearm injury to the 400 members of his local American Academy of Pediatrics chapter. Of critical importance, he gets his colleagues to frame the dangers of firearms as a public health problem: "For many health care providers this [is] quite honestly the first time that they [will] consider the issue of firearm violence as a public health issue, an epidemic of sorts."[91]

As the number of organizations a potential recruit belongs to increases, there is a greater probability that he or she will actually become a member of a social-movement organization. McAdam, McCarthy, and Zald observe that "movement organizers have long appreciated how difficult it is to recruit single, isolated individuals and they expend most of their energies mobilizing support within existing organizations."[92] A person belonging to numerous organizations is likely to be a joiner by nature and thus more susceptible to recruitment. In addition, persons belonging to many organizations are more likely to meet and interact with movement supporters. HCI, like nearly all modern organizations seeking to increase their membership, shares mailing lists with friendly organizations and uses these lists as an important recruiting tool. HCI also works closely with a variety of nonprofit organizations and by way of these joint ventures finds many recruits. Recent examples of such ventures include HCI's working with the San Diego Urban League to organize grassroots informational rallies and cooperating with the Southern Christian Leadership Conference in Birmingham, Alabama, to conduct a workshop on preventing youth violence.[93]

Attitudinal predisposition cannot be ignored when trying to understand the recruitment process. Obviously, a man who hunts and is lifelong member of both the NRA and the Republican Party, for example, would have a low predisposition to agree with the ideology and goals of the gun control movement. However, this factor easily can be overemphasized. Social scientists have long known that the link between attitude and behavior can be twisted and weak. In the 1930s, discrimination against minorities was both legally and morally acceptable to many individuals. However, a classic study of the attitude–action link conducted during this era revealed that of 251 hotel and restaurant proprietors reporting they would discriminate against a Chinese person (not serve him or her), only one actually did so when a Chinese husband–wife couple was sent to each of the establishments.[94]

Attitudes only become important in the presence of other individual-level factors that encourage movement participation, such as those noted previously. Other factors would also include *biographical availability, a personal history of prior support of other social movements,* or *suddenly felt or imposed grievances.* Biographical availability is equivalent to the amount of free time an individual has at his or her disposal. Obviously, a married individual working full-time and moonlighting at a second job who has young children and spends weekends taking care of his or her sick father in a nursing home has little time or energy left over for social-movement activity. HCI clearly recognizes that biographical availability is highly variable and gears appeals for support to match this variability.

At one extreme, in its newsletters, brochures, and other outreach literature, it entreats "If you have time on your hands (whatever the reason) you can feel free to spend it with us. We can always use a helping hand. Call …" Or "contact Handgun Control's Community Outreach department for tips on how to organize a local activists group." At the other extreme, it notes that if you have no time you can just send money. And in between, they ask for volunteer activity that takes some time and effort, but not onerously so—for example, "write a letter to the editor of your local paper," "participate in HCI events (even if that means just showing up to be part of the crowd)," "write to your state legislator," and "write a letter to the people who represent you in Congress."[95]

HCI aggressively seeks individuals with personal histories of supporting social movements and reaches out to those belonging to such diverse organizations as the Coalition for Peace Action, the Gray Panthers, the National Coalition against Domestic Violence, and Women Strike for Peace. HCI also recognizes that individuals experiencing sudden grievances are ripe for recruitment. The highest-profile example of this was the recruitment of Sarah Brady into the organization after her husband was tragically hit by a bullet intended for Ronald Reagan. In the early years of the organization, HCI staffers scoured newspapers to find incidents of gun violence and then called the victims' families. Although these staffers report that they often felt embarrassed by such a tactic and that, moreover, it was emotionally draining to listen to victims' family members pour out their profound sorrows, they kept it up because the volunteers they gleaned came to HCI with intense dedication and a willingness to work extremely hard.[96]

For example, during the early years, many such volunteers would donate money to HCI that they otherwise might have spent on Christmas gifts. Others would write all of their acquaintances, often numbering in the hundreds, and urge them to join HCI. Volunteers garnered from victims' families would also be quick to contact the media, as well as their local, state, and federal legislators, with their stories. In the words of one married couple devoting themselves to HCI—words that surely represent the sentiments of many others—"Michele's [our daughter's] death must not be in vain. We also feel that because of her death, our own lives should, and will, not be in vain."[97]

HCI continually broadens its appeals to individuals who have suffered incidences of gun violence in their families. In May 1995, HCI sponsored a Mother's Day Memorial to bring together mothers and families of gun violence victims. Fifty such mothers marched up Capitol Hill, where they delivered six five-foot tall Mother's Day cards—decorated with the photos of the lost family members—to the offices of House Speaker Newt Gingrich and Senate Majority Leader Bob Dole. The event received extensive media coverage on television (CNN, Good Morning America, the Today show) and in print (the *Los Angeles Times, New York Times,* and many other major newspapers).[98] Similarly, for Father's Day in June 1995, HCI sponsored tree-planting memorial ceremonies in Richmond and Houston, both led by fathers who had lost children to gun violence.[99]

HCI often tries to capitalize on major gun violence tragedies that can spark—in a large portion of the populace—suddenly felt anger, sorrow, fear, and zeal about the place of firearms in American society. HCI makes every effort to ensure that its interpretation of these events (too many uncontrolled guns in society create too much violence) is promoted by the media, along with a plea to do something about the situation by joining HCI or supporting in some way HCI's goals (the creation of strict national regulations on firearms).

Media reports of Patrick Purdy's massacre in Stockton, California; of George Hennard's slaughter of 22 people (and wounding of another 23) in Killen, Texas, in October 1991; and of Colin Ferguson's rampage on the Long Island Rail Road in December 1993 (5 dead, 18 wounded) are typical of this approach. For example, a *New York Times* story on the Purdy tragedy noted that "gun control advocates said that the AK-47 [that Purdy used] and similar weapons are 'built to kill large numbers of human beings quickly and efficiently.' "[100] Although HCI does not keep daily records, HCI staffers report that major gun tragedies (or near tragedies, as when Martin Duran fired an assault rifle at the White House in October 1994) are followed by spikes in membership applications and queries from the public for information.[101]

As its operations expanded in the 1980s and early 1990s, HCI broadened its structure to pursue its organizational goals more effectively. It created a political action committee (the National Handgun Control Political Action Committee) to funnel money to its favored political candidates and to handle its lobbying efforts. It created a sister corporation, the Center to Prevent Handgun Violence (CPHV), to handle its educational programs and relations with the media, as well as to encourage donations because they would be tax deductible (unlike money given to HCI proper). HCI created the Legal Action Project to pursue lawsuits against gun and ammunition manufacturers and to challenge the NRA's interpretation of the Second Amendment in the courts and in the court of public opinion (e.g., sponsoring newspaper ads and buying time on radio and television). It then formed an entertainment resources department to work with the motion picture and television industries to try to ensure that these media presented the effects of firearms realistically. It created a law enforcement relations department to work with local and national police organizations in securing their support of HCI's agenda of strict firearms regulation. It created a research center to gather and analyze gun violence data. Finally, HCI made a public outreach department to assist its supporters in starting local HCI chapters and to create liaisons and form alliances with sympathetic organizations (e.g., the Coalition to Stop Gun Violence, the League of Women Voters, the NAACP—by the winter of 1996, HCI had formed more than one hundred such alliances).

The original *incentive to act,* "we've suffered, and now we must hang together if we're to have any chance at all to realize our goals" (which is typical of most social-movement organizations in their embryonic stages of development), was supplanted, to a significant degree, by the income, prestige, and sense of personal power that come with any professional job. At its epicenter—that is, at its headquarters in Washington, D.C.—HCI leaders and staff have become bureaucrats. (Here, the term *bureaucrat* has no pejorative connotation; social scientists have long recognized that the bureaucratic organization of labor is essential to the large-scale and efficient production of goods and services.) Some of the early founders (Pete Shields and Charles Orasin) filled positions in the bureaucracy, while other founders (most notably, Mark Borinsky and Edward Welles) slowly withdrew their participation as the organization's operations became increasingly formalized and bureaucratized.

Social-movement organization goals and tactics are critical in explaining long-term sustainment and success. In trying to achieve its ultimate goal of getting strict, national-level gun regulations enacted in the United States, HCI employs eight of the nine most popular tactics displayed in figure 5.3. Social-movement organizations dedicated to the environment have found threats of public problems are important in generating public support and in recruiting activists; offering selective incentives (discounts on car rentals, life insurance, and so on) is not as critical.[102]

Accordingly, HCI and other organizations (e.g., the Coalition to Stop Gun Violence (CSGV)—the heir of NCBH) that are part of the gun control movement emphasize the human devastation associated with the widespread availability and use of firearms. They stress not only the cost in individual terms (losing a loved one to gun violence) but in social terms also (the medical costs associated with firearm violence; the judicial-system costs of gun crime). Anyone requesting information from HCI or CSGV is sent flyers and pamphlets in which a barrage of gun violence statistics (murders, suicides, accidents, medical costs, criminal costs) are reeled off. Thus gun control groups, especially HCI, have achieved sustained membership growth by demonstrating the harm firearms cause.

HCI did well in *exploiting the communication technologies* of the 1980s but not (as of early 1997) of the 1990s. HCI uses the mail to communicate with and expand its membership—not only to ask for donations and membership dues but to alert members to local, state, and

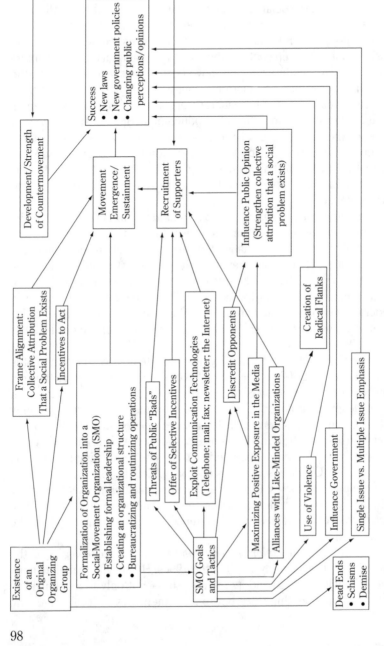

Figure 5.3. Social-Movement Theory: Medial-Level Constructs

national legislative activities that relate to gun control. Members in Rhode Island, for example, will be notified if a momentous gun bill is before the state legislature, so that they can write or call their representatives and even attend committee hearings that are open to the public. HCI also uses the telephone and fax machine to make urgent appeals or notifications. Via desktop publishing, HCI creates three newsletters (*The Outreach, Rx for Gun Violence,* and *Legal Action Report*) to communicate with its members. Where HCI has not kept up, especially when compared to its arch rival the NRA, is in getting on the Internet. As of February 1997, HCI had no Internet address (apart from the personal addresses of a few staffers) and no World Wide Web home page. Given its middle- and upper-middle-class membership bases, this is an especially egregious deficiency. However, it is not one that has gone unrecognized, and the organization expects to have both a home page and e-mail system in place by summer 1997.

HCI works hard to *maximize "positive" media exposure.* The organization regularly holds press conferences, puts out press releases, volunteers as a source of expert opinion on gun issues for major news organizations, buys radio and television time, and advertises heavily in nationally important newspapers such as the *New York Times,* the *Los Angeles Times, USA Today,* and the *Washington Post.* Moreover, for many years, the media has by and large been considered a friend of the gun control movement and an enemy of the NRA and its sister organizations. Big-city newspapers report on gun crime and gun violence every day; this, combined with the liberal leanings of many news analysts, reporters, and editors on social issues,[103] produces an antigun bias in reporting, editorials, opinion/editorial commentary, and letters to the editor (characterized by the progun side as "the hot air of the anti-gun media"[104]). Recent editorials in the *Providence Journal-Bulletin* and the *New York Times* are typical:

President Clinton rightly senses that, at long last, the momentum exists to do something about guns.... Reducing the number of firearms in circulation, and the amount and variety of ammunition available, will have an immediate effect on the violence in a way that addressing root causes, while important, will not. For quite simply, as Dr. David Satcher, the new head of the Centers for Disease Control, recently put it, "anything we can do to get guns out of the hands of children and out of homes would reduce the fatality rate." We hope the President's courage to take on this issue will not desert him, and that he will press his recently announced plan to introduce new gun-control measures early next year. It is important that he seize this hour, in which pubic concern has crystallized and the Congress is inclined toward action, to get tougher restrictions enacted.[105]

The abandonment of the NRA by law enforcement officials is one of the most striking gun-control developments of the past decade. Those officials, like many Americans, are tired of the NRA's willful misreading of the Second Amendment and its guarantee of the right to keep and bear arms for the purpose of maintaining state militias. As Sylvester Daughtry Jr., a North Carolina police chief, told Congress in the spring, the idea that control of deadly weapons in the streets restricts the rights of sportsmen is a "simplistic and dreamy distinction." The higher goal for law enforcement and the average citizen, he observed, is to "do something about this gun madness."[106]

Handgun Control Incorporated also uses the media to demonize the NRA and, in general, to *discredit its opponents*. For example, in spring 1995, HCI ran an expensive advertisement in 10 high-profile newspapers (including the *New York Times* and the *Washington Post*) denigrating the NRA's interpretation of the Second Amendment:[107]

For years, the National Rifle Association has spread the myth that gun control laws violate the Second Amendment. Now self-styled "citizen militias" invoke the Second Amendment as they stockpile weapons and train for warfare against what they perceive as a "tyrannical" federal government. The NRA declares that the paramilitary activity of these groups is an exercise of their "right to keep and bear arms." Echoing the extremist rhetoric of the "militias," an NRA official has called the Second Amendment "a loaded gun ... held to the head of government." This is a perversion of the Constitution.... Because laws regulating firearms do not interfere with the modern militia [the National Guard], no gun control law has ever been overturned by the federal courts on Second Amendment grounds. That's why former Supreme Court Chief Justice Warren Burger has called the NRA's Second Amendment propaganda a "fraud on the American public." ... It's time for the NRA to stop its Second Amendment fraud.[108]

In addition to the NRA and its smaller progun allies (e.g., Gun Owners of America), HCI is quick to use the media to discredit its opponents in Congress. Favorite targets in 1995 were House Speaker Newt Gingrich and Bob Barr, chair of the House Task Force on Firearms, which conservative Republicans created in late 1994 to marshal efforts toward repealing the assault-weapons-ban sections of the 1994 Violent Crime Control and Law Enforcement Act.

HCI sees its future success as closely linked with the *alliances* it can make with organizations sympathetic to its goals. In 1995, HCI established contacts with 108 national organizations, representing—according to HCI—140 million Americans (among the better known organizations were the American Association of Retired Persons, the Gray Panthers, the American Medical Association, the NAACP, the National Association of Public Hospitals, the United States Catholic Conference, and the United States Conference of Mayors). Calling its alliance-forming drive the "Campaign to Protect Sane Gun Laws," HCI secured from each organization a pledge "to oppose the gun lobby's efforts to repeal sensible gun laws such as the Brady Law and the assault weapons ban."[109] The campaign would let "members of Congress now clearly understand that the more than 70% of their constituents who support banning assault weapons *will not tolerate* the repeal of that ban."[110]

A similar pledge-signing drive was the strategy of the Methodist Church back in 1975 when it created the National Coalition to Ban Handguns. One reason HCI (then still called the National Council to Control Handguns [NCCH]) broke off from the coalition was that Mark Borinsky and Edward Welles believed such a strategy has little political value[111] (as noted earlier, the other key reason was the reformulated goal of NCCH to seek *controls* over handguns instead of their total *banning*). That is, all advocacy organizations have many goals that they say they support, but, in truth, this support is only nominal—no one in the organization seriously expects it to expend many resources to obtain the goal. However, in 1975 there was nothing equivalent to HCI as it had become by 1995, and the many organizations signing their names to this particular cause lacked the champion they needed for the political value of their signing to be fully realized. This particular saga is still unfolding, but it can be expected that HCI will deftly use the imprimaturs of the 108 organizations as one of its key weapons in battling the NRA for influence on Capitol Hill in the late 1990s.

The *radical flanks* in the gun control movement are HCI's allies CSGV (the Coalition to Stop Gun Violence—formerly, the NCBH) and the Violence Policy Center (VPC), both headquartered in Washington, D.C. Radical flanks (social-movement organizations [SMOs] in the movement that have extremist goals) can benefit more moderate SMOs, ultimately giving them more influence than they would otherwise have had.[112] CSGV and VPC are *ban* organizations; that is, they believe in the outright banning of handguns, as in Japan, the Netherlands, and Spain. Philanthropic foundations[113] and congressional representatives interested in gun control have ended up concentrating their resources and efforts on HCI because of its more moderate goal of *strictly controlling,* rather than outlawing, handguns and other firearms.

Because public opinion has always been squarely against the outright ban of handguns (see figure 4.2), most pro–gun control legislators have chosen to work with HCI to maximize the probability of success. One result has been to concentrate the movement's resources in a single organization (HCI) and thereby derive economic and political efficiencies (e.g., the easier development of strategy and the easier coordination of tactics; fewer well-funded SMOs means fewer bureaucracies to support overall). VPC has a staff of 2, CSGV a staff of 7, and HCI a staff of 44 full-time workers and several dozen part-timers.[114] Although HCI works with VPC and CSGV from time to time on Capitol Hill, the jealousy of the smaller organizations is sometimes hard to hide. Here is VPC Executive Director Josh Sugarmann's analysis of why HCI's efforts will be vain in the long run:

Ironically, despite the genuine hatred that each organization feels for the other, HCI and the NRA share a similar view of the nature of gun violence. Neither sees the handgun itself as inherently the problem, but views violence as stemming from the weapons being in the "wrong" hands. The NRA states its case with the familiar bumper sticker slogan: "Guns Don't Kill, People Do." HCI's catchphrase, "Working to Keep Handguns Out of the Wrong Hands," clarifies the NRA's argument into "Guns Don't Kill, *Bad* People Do."

HCI defines the "wrong hands" as minors, criminals, drunks, drug users, and the mentally incompetent. Yet this universe, by its own definition, is small. ... Like the NRA, HCI is quick to paint handgun violence as a "crime" issue and promises that its legislative remedies will make it hard for these "wrong hands" to hold a handgun.... By framing the issue in terms of "crime," HCI and the NRA have created a situation where, no matter which organization eventually triumphs, little will be accomplished to end the killing.... Crime is merely the most publicized aspect of the widespread public health problem created by the easy availability of handguns. The vast majority of handgun deaths are suicides—about 12,000 per year. And although one out of ten who attempt suicide will kill themselves no matter what, for most the will to die lasts briefly. The success or failure of an attempt rests primarily on the lethality of the means employed. Pills and razor blades are inefficient and allow for second thoughts.

Handguns do the job to near perfection.... [Moreover,] for all murder victims, more than half [know] their killers. Fifteen percent [occur] between family members, while 39 percent [involve] acquaintances.... In other words, whenever handguns are around, the "right hands" have a nasty tendency to turn into the "wrong hands." ... That HCI suffers from institutional schizophrenia is illustrated by the fact that the organization and its foundation, the Center to Prevent Handgun Violence, consistently acknowledge the damage done by legal handgun possession and their uselessness as self-defense tools, yet are unwilling to endorse handgun banning.... At times it seems as if the effectiveness of HCI's proposals doesn't matter to the organization anymore. The purpose for which the movement was created—saving lives—has been superseded by a new goal: beating the NRA.[115]

Three alliances—those with law enforcement, education, and medicine—that HCI has managed to create deserve special mention. Because of the NRA's traditional role in sponsoring gun safety classes—and in promoting the responsible use of firearms in general—the organization long enjoyed a cozy relationship with law enforcement personnel and their organizations. However, as the NRA became increasingly stridently opposed to *any and every* form of gun control (including mandatory safety classes), it began to alienate significant portions of the law enforcement community. The last straw was passage of the 1986 Firearms Owners' Protection Act (also known as the McClure–Volkmer act), which removed record-keeping requirements for ammunitions dealers and allowed mail-order sales of rifles, shotguns, and ammunition to resume. The NRA lobbied hard for the passage of this act.

In the words of a former executive director of the International Association of Chiefs of Police (the premier law enforcement professional association in the country), "after [McClure–Volkmer], many in law enforcement began to question not only the motives and tactics, but the basic integrity of the NRA."[116] These individuals and organizations were ripe for recruitment into the gun control movement, and HCI went about this task proactively through its law enforcement relations department. Eventually, most mainline professional police associations—including the International Association of Chiefs of Police, the Police Executive Research Forum, the National Fraternal Order of Police, the National Organization of Black Law Enforcement Executives, the National Troopers Coalition, the International Brotherhood of Police Officers, the Law Enforcement Officers Association, the

National Sheriffs Association, and the National Association of Police Organizations—were brought over to the gun control side.

Through the Center to Prevent Handgun Violence, HCI has established strong ties with education. CPHV's flagship educational program is Straight Talk about Risks (STAR). It is aimed for youth in grades prekindergarten through 12. STAR materials are available in English and Spanish, and they include classroom activities, posters, handouts, videos, and a bibliography of supplemental resources. During 1993 and 1994, STAR was implemented in selected schools and youth agencies in 30 cities; CPHV staff trained more than 2,000 teachers in the STAR curriculum, and more than 150,000 students went through the program. Both STAR and HCI's political lobbying receive strong endorsements from the two largest professional organizations for teachers, the National Education Association and the American Federation of Teachers.[117]

Almost all major medical associations have been brought into the gun control movement's fold. CPHV's primary medical education program is Steps to Prevent Firearm Injury (STOP). It is aimed at getting pediatric health professionals to counsel parents and adolescents about the risks of guns in the home. STOP materials, available in English and Spanish, include brochures, posters, audiocassettes, and a monograph. In the early 1990s, STOP materials were delivered to more than 6,500 pediatricians. Follow-up studies reveal "widespread user satisfaction by pediatricians and their high degree of willingness to provide specific counseling to parents about removal and safe storage of guns."[118]

STOP and HCI political-lobbying efforts have received strong support from the American Academy of Pediatrics. More generally, the American Medical Association (AMA),[119] most state medical associations (Georgia's being an exception),[120] the U.S. Public Health Service (and the Surgeon General),[121] and the federal Centers for Disease Control[122] have all endorsed the idea of strong regulations on guns to prevent the carnage related to firearms that the health care system witnesses daily. For example, in what was one of the most highly publicized editorials ever appearing in the *Journal of the American Medical Association,* the official AMA position on gun control was stated as follows:

Automobiles, intended to be a means of transportation, when used inappropriately frequently become lethal weapons and kill human beings. Firearms are intended to be lethal weapons. When used inappropriately in peace time, they, too, frequently kill human beings.

... The right to own or operate a motor vehicle carries with it certain responsibilities. Among them are that the operator meet certain criteria:

- be a certain age and physical/mental condition;
- be identifiable as owner or operator;
- be able to demonstrate knowledge and skill in operating the motor vehicle safely;
- be subject to performance monitoring; and
- be willing to forfeit the right to operate or own a vehicle if these responsibilities are abrogated.

We propose that the right to own or operate a firearm carries with it the same prior conditions, namely that the owner and operator of a firearm also meet specific criteria:

- be a certain age and physical/mental condition;
- be able to demonstrate knowledge and skill in proper use of that firearm;
- be monitored in the firearm's use; and
- forfeit the right to own or operate the firearm if these conditions are abrogated.

These restrictions should apply uniformly to all firearms and to all U.S. inhabitants across all states through a system of gun registration and licensing for gun owners and users. No grandfather clauses should be allowed.... We can wait no longer to act.[123]

The alliances with law enforcement, education, and medicine, as well as those made through the Campaign to Protect Sane Gun Laws, fit tactically into HCI's strategy to *influence government*. This effect is sought through three major venues. First, HCI's political action committee funnels money to its "A"-rated candidates in congressional election races. (Actually, HCI lets the NRA do the work—the NRA's "F" candidates become HCI's "A" candidates, and HCI distributes to its membership the NRA report card on candidates; the NRA's ratings are based on a comprehensive examination of candidates' past voting and commentary on gun control.) Second, HCI lobbies Congress intensively, and as part of this effort provides research and support to legislators willing to propose gun control legislation (such as Howard Metzenbaum and Charles Schumer). Whenever possible, HCI brings along one or more of its major organizational allies when venturing onto Capitol Hill to testify at committee hearings or perform related lobbying work.

Third, HCI fights for gun control in the courts. It files friends-of-the-court (*amicus*) briefs in support of gun laws being challenged (most challenges being instituted by the NRA or one of its sister organizations, or by an individual who has NRA/sister organization support).[124] It also takes more proactive measures—offering counsel to the victims of gun violence and suing gun manufacturers for negligence. In this area, one highly publicized case is HCI's legal representation of families of victims in the July 1993 massacre at 101 California Street, where a lone gunman used two TEC-DC9 assault pistols to kill eight people and wound six others in a high-rise San Francisco office building. The families are suing the manufacturer of the TEC pistols, Intratec, on the basis of "common law negligences and ultrahazardous activity." HCI lawyers are arguing that "the manufacture and sale to the general public of an assault pistol like the TEC-DC9 violated Intratec's duty of care to the general public not to sell guns that are especially well-suited for mass killing and ill-suited for legitimate sporting or self-defense use." Further, the lawyers contend that "the sale of these guns to the general public is an unusual activity which exposes the community to an extraordinary risk of harm."[125]

A second highly publicized case is HCI's filing of a lawsuit against Beretta U.S.A. Corp. On May 29, 1994, Kenzo Dix was playing at the home of a friend in Berkeley, California. The friend found his parent's 9-mm Beretta handgun and removed its ammunition clip. Thinking he had an unloaded gun in his hand, the friend pointed the Beretta at Kenzo and pulled the trigger—tragically unaware that a bullet still remained in the chamber. Kenzo was killed. The HCI suit contends that the design of the Beretta presents a risk of grave danger because foreseeable users, like inquisitive children, do not understand that a bullet is often hidden in the gun's firing chamber, even though the ammunition clip has been removed. Further, the suit alleges that gun manufacturers such as Beretta have long had the ability to make handguns safer by designing them so that they will fire only in the hands of an authorized user. Numerous devices to accomplish this have been available for years. Among them are combination push-button locks fitted on the pistol grip of a handgun (a shooter must know the combination of the lock before he or she can fire it) and the "Magna-Trigger," which prevents anyone other than the wearer of a magnetized ring from firing the handgun. Both the Intratec and Beretta lawsuits have survived initial attempts to have them thrown out of court.[126]

In discussions with the early founders of HCI as to why it grew to dominate the gun control movement, while other organizations formed for the same purpose in the same era (namely NCBH) achieved considerably less success, HCI's having a *single-issue as opposed to a multiple-issue emphasis* is often cited. The 30 organizations that formed the NCBH coalition had many goals other than the control of firearms: To paraphrase Edward Welles (one of HCI's founders), this was just one of the things they were after and not one that they were necessarily prepared to follow through on.[127]

In his path-breaking study of social-movement success in American history, Gamson found that single-issue SMOs had much higher success rates than their counterparts pursuing many goals.[128] In the specific case of HCI, having a single-issue focus not only has allowed it to concentrate its resources on gun control alone, but it has shaped its membership in such a way as to make it more powerful than it otherwise would be. That is, as noted earlier, HCI has always made its strongest appeal to individuals whose lives have been traumatized by gun violence. Losing a child or other loved one to gunfire can come to dominate a person's day-to-day thinking and life choices. Recruits from families victimized by gun violence are often willing to throw themselves fully into the gun control movement and its goals. As past HCI president Pete Shields observed, "we came to see that in order to build a political constituency for handgun controls powerful enough to neutralize the NRA, we must begin with those who [have] been personally affected by the issue—the victims of handgun violence."[129]

The Countermovement's Strength and Strategies

The *development/strength-of-countermovement* factor (figure 5.3) has been critical in limiting the overall success of the gun control movement. As noted in chapter 4, public opinion on gun control is strong, reasonably well informed, and highly visible: Most Americans see a connection between the high levels of gun trauma (murder, accidents, suicides) in the United States and the nation's high prevalence of firearms. Moreover, most Americans want strict, national gun regulations on par with those of other industrialized democracies.

That this desire has not been translated into law is largely a function of the NRA-dominated countermovement. In the words of political scientist Robert Spitzer, "the NRA provides the prototypical example of single-issue interest politics at work.... [It is] a highly motivated, intense minority operating effectively in the interest-group milieu." Such a minority "will usually prevail in a political contest over a larger, relatively apathetic majority; and it is easier to prevent policy enactment than cause it. With the exception of McClure–Volkmer [the 1986 Firearm Owners' Protection Act], the NRA's political tack has been opposition to policy enactment."[130]

The size of the NRA's budget and membership has always been many magnitudes greater than HCI's; for example, HCI's total operating budget in 1992 was less than $6 million, but that same year, just one of the NRA's divisions, the Political Victory Fund, spent $6.8 million (most income for both organizations comes from membership dues and contributions; HCI has 400,000 members—at $15 for dues this would produce a minimum income of $6 million; the NRA has 3.2 million members who pay $35 a year, producing a minimum of $112 million a year).[131] When political opportunity favors the NRA—a Republican president or at least one house in Congress in which Republicans are in a majority—it is a powerful foe. The example given previously, whereby the NRA thwarted a proposed ban on Saturday Night Specials in the House Judiciary Committee, was repeated dozens of times between 1976 and 1992, and again after November 1994 (when Republicans took control of both houses of Congress).[132]

When the political fortunes of national politics swung toward the gun control movement in the 1988–1994 period (as described earlier), the NRA began concentrating its efforts at the state level. It helped to get right-to-carry legislation enacted in 28 states, developing or amending laws that made it relatively easy for ordinary citizens to carry concealed weapons (namely handguns). The organization also fought successfully in 42 states to enact preemption laws, prohibiting local governments from passing their own gun control laws. When the New NRA saw its support from police organizations waning, it began an aggressive campaign to recruit law enforcement and public-safety officers so that by 1995 it could tout that more than 150,000 NRA members worked in this profession ("local, state, federal, private security").[133] When HCI began an aggressive program to form alliances with sympathetic organizations (e.g., the National Education Association), the NRA stepped up promotion of its Business Alliance campaign—gathering under its fold hundreds of small businesses (mostly firearm related, such as gun shops and shooting ranges).

When it became clear that HCI and the gun control movement were going to have the sympathy of most members of the mass media (the NRA estimates that only 4 percent of network gun control reports are progun[134]), the NRA began aggressive mass communication efforts on its own. It began its own weekly radio show (available in most of the nation); it was one of the first organizations in Washington to make full use of the Internet (its electronic bulletin boards, listservs, and World Wide Web home page are models for other interest groups to emulate); and it conducted mass mailings of its various gun-facts sheets to promote its point of view on the role of firearms in American society. The NRA has been particularly sensitive to the accusation that it is a front for the U.S. firearms industry (a major theme in Josh Sugarmann's *NRA: Money, Firepower, Fear*) and widely circulates don't-buy-HCI-lies position papers denying that it has any motivation to be politically active other than to protect the right of all Americans (except violent criminals) to keep and bear arms.[135]

There is no doubt that the NRA knows how to work Capitol Hill: In the words of one *Washington Post* editorial, "few lobbies have so mastered the marble halls and concrete canyons of Washington," and according to the *New York Times,* the gun lobby is "the most persistent and resourceful of all single-issue groups."[136] Moreover, extensive empirical analyses of congressional voting reveal that legislators receiving NRA PAC money vote progun (HCI PAC money produces the same sympathetic effect, that is, its donees tend to vote antigun).[137] However, in elections, the NRA's power is more questionable. Whether progun or antigun candidates get elected in the first place seems to be weakly related, at best, to PAC support from either the NRA or HCI.[138] Forces more diverse and greater than the campaign gifts or communications with members of a single-issue group determine election outcomes. In his analysis of congressional elections in the early 1970s, political commentator Robert Sherrill observes that an "all-powerful" NRA

is the legend, but what are the facts? Where are the fallen bodies of the politicians who opposed the NRA? When you ask for specifics you are asked in turn to accept assumptions. Should the NRA be given credit for the defeat of Senator Joseph Tydings of Maryland in 1970? It claims credit, and points to the half-million anti-Tydings brochures, the thirty full-page ads, the radio spots in Maryland's duck-hunting neck of the state which the riflemen paid for to oppose Tydings' reelection. The riflemen also take credit for the defeats, the same year, of Senators Albert Gore of Tennessee, Charles Goodell of New York, and Tom Dodd of Connecticut. It is highly unlikely that these scalps belong on the NRA's belt. There is no evidence that the gun lobby played a significant role in their defeats. Each of these losers had to contend with a number of emotional forces that year, not just the gun crowd. Tydings had lost popularity with liberals because of his "no-knock" crime-control bill; and he had been grossly abused by a story planted with *Life* shortly before the election which unfairly charged him with conflict of interest. Gore was being hounded by conservatives of Tennessee for his antiwar stand and for his civil rights moderation. As for Dodd, he was under such a heavy cloud—having just been censured by the Senate for pilfering campaign funds—that he could scarcely be seen. And if the lobby was so potent as it claims to have been, then why did it not also defeat a number of other Senators who had voted for the 1968 [Gun Control] Act and yet who won reelection in 1970, some of them very easily, from states heavy with hunters? [e.g., Edward Kennedy, Philip Hart, John Pastore, and Hugh Scott][139]

Systematic empirical assessments of 1980s congressional elections reveal that the NRA's record was "spotty." The NRA made its greatest campaign contributions in safe districts—that is, in districts where incumbents were favored to win heavily and actually did so. In open districts, where no incumbent ran, "NRA candidates lost in over half the cases."[140] The NRA spent heavily in the congressional races of 1992 and 1994 (a combined sum of more than ten million dollars); in 1994, 80 percent of NRA candidates for Congress won, their greatest electoral success ever.

However, it is questionable how much of the success of the candidates it backed was due to NRA support. First, the 1994 elections were midterm (congressional elections held in the middle of a president's term), and with only one exception (1934), in every midterm election since 1862, the president's party has lost seats (expectations raised in a presidential campaign are never met and voters express their disappointment in the midterm elections).[141] This phenomenon in American political life was especially notable in 1994, since Bill Clinton's "approval ratings for the first two years of his administration were the lowest of any president over the same span since polling data became available."[142]

More importantly, the ascendancy of conservative politicians has been driven by a shift in public opinion on the role of government that has been evolving over the past two decades—a shift in which "Americans have become more skeptical about [government's] efficacy, less inclined to agree when a politician approaches them saying, in effect, 'We have a terrible problem, and this new program is what's needed.' The new mood of doubt or skepticism about extending the modern state ... doesn't posit a certain partisan winner—though in the short-term it has evidently weakened the Democrats' position."[143] Moreover, as already noted, because being anti–gun control does not cohere with public opinion, the NRA tends to attack candidates they consider as antigun on other issues (e.g., not keeping campaign promises and ethics).[144]

In sum, between 1976 and 1996, the NRA developed into a powerful countermovement to HCI and the gun control movement. The New NRA takes on HCI at every turn in the political road, from elections of legislators to the fate of their proposed legislation as it is debated in committee and on the open floors of state and federal legislative bodies. Because the NRA has evolved a no-compromise approach to politics, there is no motivation on either side of the gun control debate to work together toward the regulation of firearms in American society, as was done in the 1930s-to-1970s era, when the NRA cooperated with various pro–gun control legislators and other government officials (e.g., from the Justice Department or the National Health Institutes). What is clear is that both movements, representing the pro- and the anticontrol philosophies, are now large enough and well funded enough to take advantage of the changing winds of political opportunity and, indeed, to partly direct these winds.

The Future of the Gun Control Movement

Several features of American society and politics ensure that the gun control movement will continue to survive and very likely thrive in the decade to come. First, America is awash in guns—223 million rifles, shotguns, and pistols as of 1993, with four to five million new firearms (half of them pistols) being added to the total each year.[145] Because guns don't wear out, the total number of firearms in the United States will exceed the size of its population in the not-too-distant future. Easy availability of firearms—through both legal and illegal means—is a fact of contemporary American life.

Second, crime rates in the United States have been falling for the past decade, largely in response to the baby boom generation growing up (youth and crime are highly correlated). However, the children of the baby boom produced a baby boomlet, and individuals in this cohort—40 million strong—are now hitting their teens, and street crime of all types is expected to rise in response. These two forces, youth and easy firearm availability, will propel gun violence forward.

Such violence will undoubtedly receive heavy media coverage, which will almost assuredly be slanted toward the procontrol side of the gun debate (as noted earlier, those in the media overwhelmingly support gun control). Sympathetic media coverage will keep HCI and its agenda for strict gun control in the limelight, and it would therefore be expected that membership rates and donations will remain high, if not grow outright. On the other side, the NRA's head start in membership and resources (as of 1996, about an 8 to 1 advantage in membership and at least a 10 to 1 advantage in financial assets) will allow it to maintain a powerful presence on Capitol Hill no matter how much HCI expands over the next decade.

The trump card in this war over gun regulation will be the political makeup of the Congress and the presidency. As shown in this chapter, each side has made its greatest gains when political opportunity favored it. A conservative president and at least one house of Congress that is conservative favor the NRA and the progun side. In contrast, a liberal president and a liberal majority in at least one house favor HCI and the antigun side. Any other combination—liberal president/conservative Congress or conservative president/liberal Congress—will likely produce a standoff; the strong gun control legislation of 1993–1994 (the Brady law and the assault-weapons ban) will be neither dismantled nor built upon. With a Republican-controlled Congress and a Democratic president, we can expect a standoff through the year 2000.

Nevertheless, the key political trend in the past 25 years has been toward conservatism. If the trend continues, and there is little reason to doubt that it will do so, then we might well find a conservative Republican in the White House in 2001. If this scenario unfolds, success for the gun control movement will be defined by what it does not lose (e.g., the assault-weapons ban) rather than by what it gains. However, the movement will be in a much better financial and organizational position to put up a good fight. Pitiably, if history is our guide, it will take another horrendous incident of gun violence ("disgruntled employee slays 26 coworkers, wounds 30 more") to assure even limited success.

On the other hand, if some series of quirks keeps the presidency in the hands of the Democrats and elects a liberal Congress at the century's turn, then it would not be surprising to see a good portion, if not all, of Brady II (described previously) enacted, placing American gun regulations on par with those in its peer nations. There would be a convergence of forces that has never occurred in U.S. history: a liberal Congress, a liberal president, public opinion strongly favoring gun control, and a powerful and well-organized gun control movement to counteract the NRA and others that prefer the status quo, that is, weak and ineffective gun laws.

Notes

Chapter One

1.   Gary Kleck, *Point Blank: Guns and Violence in America* (New York: Aldine de Gruyter, 1991), 153.

2.   As quoted in Thomas J. Morgan, "United States Is the Most Violent Society," *Providence Journal-Bulletin,* November 8, 1995, p. C5.

3.   As quoted in A. J. Hostetler, "Guns Cost One Million Life-Years CDC Says," *Providence Journal-Bulletin,* August 26, 1994, p. A-12.

4.   James Lindgren and Franklin E. Zimring, "Regulation of Guns," in *Encyclopedia of Crime and Justice,* ed. Sanford H. Kadish (New York: The Free Press, 1983), 836–41.

5.   Assault with a gun is two and a half to five times more likely to cause death than a similar attack with a knife, the next most dangerous weapon. See Philip J. Cook, "The Effect of Gun Availability on Robbery and Robbery Murder: A Cross-Section Study of Fifteen Cities," *Hearings before the Subcommittee on Crime of the Committee on the Judiciary, House of Representatives,* 95th Cong., 2d sess., May 4 and 18, 1978 (Washington, D.C.: Government Printing Office), 281–311; George D. Newton Jr. and Franklin E. Zimring, *Firearms and Violence in American Life: A Staff Report Submitted to the National Commission on the Causes and Prevention of Violence* (Washington, D.C.: Government Printing Office, 1969); and Lindgren and Zimring, "Regulation of Guns," p. 837.

6.   New members of Handgun Control Incorporated are sent a *Firearm Facts* sheet. In the 1995 sheet, the first five facts listed are

these: (1) "In 1992, 37,502 Americans were killed with **firearms**, in homicides, suicides, and accidents. That's 103 American men, women, and children every day!" (2) "Handguns were used to murder 14,204 people in this country in 1993—up more than 5% from 1992." (3) "18,152 Americans took their own lives with firearms in 1992." (4) "In 1992, 1,409 people were accidentally killed with firearms." (5) "Every day, 15 children, aged 19 and under, are killed with guns." (Sources: F.B.I. Uniform Crime Reports; National Center for Health Statistics.)

7.   *Ten Myths about Gun Control* (Fairfax, Va.: NRA Institute for Legislative Action, 1994), 9.

8.   The correlation coefficient (r) is commonly used to summarize the strength of the relationship between two variables. It can vary between -1 and +1. As r approaches zero, the relationship becomes increasingly less significant. As r approaches either –1 or +1, the relationship becomes increasingly stronger. The sign (+ or –) of the coefficient indicates only the direction of the relationship, not its strength. Thus, a correlation between X and Y of –.5 and a correlation between X and Z of +.5 are equal in strength. The sign merely denotes the direction of the relationship. For positive relationships, the variables are changing in the same direction (e.g., increases in one variable are associated with increases in the other variable). For negative relationships, the variables are changing in opposite directions (e.g., increases in one variable are associated with decreases in the other variable). Correlation coefficients in the social sciences tend to be small (an absolute value of less than .5), so those at the bottom of table 1.1 would be considered remarkably strong. Consult any elementary statistics book for a discussion of correlation. See, for example, Michael Malec, *Essential Statistics for Social Research,* 2d ed. (Boulder, Colo.: Westview Press, 1993), chapter 11.

9.   Po-Han Lin, "Pro-Gun Control FAQ, Version 1.5," posted on the Internet as http://www.webcom.com/~centrnv/gunfaq.html.

10.   Kleck, *Point Blank*, pp. 188–89. Also see James D. Wright, "Second Thoughts about Gun Control," *Public Interest*, Vol. 91 (Spring 1988), 23–39.

11.   For a detailed breakdown of murder rates by race, age, and gender, see F. Landis Mackellar and Machiko Yanagishita, *Homicide in the United States: Who's at Risk?* (Washington, D.C.: Population Reference Bureau, 1995); for a discussion of rising rates of gun violence in the African-American community, see Lisa D. Bastian and Bruce M. Taylor, "Young Black Male Victims," *Bureau of Justice Statistics Crime*

Data Brief, National Crime Victimization Survey, NCJ-147004 (Washington, D.C.: Bureau of Justice Statistics, U.S. Department of Justice, December 1994).

12. James D. Wright, Joseph F. Sheley, and M. Dwayne Smith, "Kids, Guns, and Killing Fields," *Society* 30 (November–December 1992), 84–89.

13. Robert J. Cottrol and Raymond T. Diamond, "The Second Amendment: Toward an Afro-Americanist Reconsideration," *Georgetown Law Journal* 80 (December 1991): 359. The NRA distributes copies of this article free of charge to its membership.

14. Josh Sugarmann, *National Rifle Association: Money, Firepower, and Fear* (Washington, D.C.: National Press Books, 1992), 21.

15. For academic discussions of the rampant rise in gun availability and use in urban America see Charles M. Callahan and Frederick P. Rivara, "Urban High School Youth and Handguns," *Journal of the American Medical Association* 267 (June 10, 1992): 3038–42; Charles S. Clark, "Youth Gangs," *CQ Researcher* 1 (October 11, 1991): 753–76; Charles S. Clark, "Suburban Crime," *CQ Researcher* 3 (September 3, 1993): 769–92; *Drugs, Crime, and the Justice System—A National Report from the Bureau of Justice Statistics, NCJ-133652* (Washington, D.C.: Government Printing Office, December 1992); Sarah Glazer, "Violence in Schools," *CQ Researcher* 2 (September 11, 1992): 785–808; Cheryl L. Maxson and Malcolm W. Klein, "Street Gang Violence: Twice as Great or Half as Great?" in *Gangs in America,* ed. C. Ronald Huff (Newbury Park, Calif.: Sage, 1990), 71–100; Mark A. Kleiman and Kerry Smith, "State and Local Drug Enforcement: In Search of a Strategy," in *Drugs and Crime,* ed. Michael H. Tonry and James Q. Wilson (Chicago: University of Chicago Press, 1990), 69–108; Tom McEwen, *National Assessment Program: 1994 Survey Results* (Washington, D.C.: National Institute of Justice, U.S. Department of Justice, June 1995); *1991 Murder Toll: Initial Projections,* U.S. Senate, Committee on the Judiciary, Majority Staff Report (Washington, D.C.: Government Printing Office, 1991); and Joseph F. Sheley and Victoria E. Brewer, "Possession and Carrying of Firearms among Suburban Youth," *Public Health Reports* 110 (January–February 1995): 18–26. For highly readable journalistic accounts that incorporate data from the National Center for Health Statistics and the National Education Association, see James Brady, "Taking Aim at Guns," *Providence Journal-Bulletin,* April 4, 1992, p. A-12; Jon D. Hull, "A Boy and His Gun," *Time* (August 2, 1993): 20–27; and Rod Norland,

"Deadly Lessons," *Newsweek* (March 9, 1992): 22–30. For a highly personalized and persuasive account of the rapid rise of guns that began in the inner city in the mid-1980s, see Geoffrey Canada, *Fist, Stick, Knife, Gun: A Personal History of Violence in America* (Boston: Beacon Press, 1995).

16.   See Gary Kleck, "Gun Ownership and Crime," *Canadian Medical Association Journal* 149 (December 15, 1993): 1773–74; Kleck, *Point Blank*, p. 153; David B. Kopel and the various authors in his *Guns: Who Should Have Them?* (Amherst, N.Y.: Prometheus Books, 1995); and Alan J. Lizotte and David J. Bordua, "Firearms Ownership for Sport and Protection: Two Divergent Models," *American Sociological Review* 45 (April 1980): 229–44. Anecdotal evidence supporting the notion that the causal path runs from violence to gun prevalence, and not vice versa, abounds. See, for example, "Recent Mass Shootings and Talk of Further Controls Have Sent Many People to the Nearest Firearms Dealer," *New York Times,* as reprinted in the *Providence Journal-Bulletin,* December 19, 1993, p. A-3; and Jim Wright, "Gun Control? How about Enforcing Some People-Control Laws," *Providence Journal-Bulletin,* November 21, 1993, p. I-13. However, James DeFronzo's analysis of General Social Survey data led him to conclude that "the findings do not support claims that the fear of crime motivates increased handgun ownership" (p. 331); see his "Fear of Crime and Handgun Ownership," *Criminology* 17 (November 1979): 331–39.

17.   The degree to which poverty increased in the last decade is in dispute. However, the graphic on page 119 starkly reveals the enormous and growing gap between median family income and the federal poverty cutoff for four-person families.

For a cogent explanation of the relationship between poverty and violent crime, see William Julius Wilson, *The Truly Disadvantaged: The Inner City, the Underclass, and Public Policy* (Chicago: University of Chicago Press, 1987), 22–26. Also see Elliott Currie, *Reckoning: Drugs, the Cities, and the American Future* (New York: Hill and Wang, 1993).

18.   See Joseph F. Sheley and James D. Wright, *In the Line of Fire: Youth, Guns, and Violence in Urban America* (Hawthorne, N.Y.: Aldine de Gruyter, 1995), chapters 1, 7, and 8.

19.   Eighteen studies of pre-1990s U.S. data have been conducted on the correlation between gun prevalence and violent crime (both cross-sectionally and across time). The findings of these studies

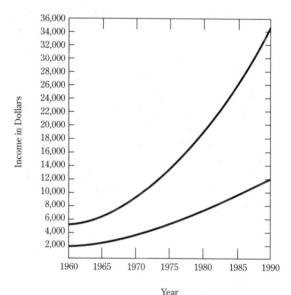

Year

Top line: Median Income for a U.S. Family; Bottom line: Poverty Cutoff
for a 4-Person Family. *Source: Statistical Abstract of the United States, 1992*

Growing Gap between Median Family Income and the Federal Poverty Cutoff

are at odds, however, and it is unclear whether the correlation is sta-
tistically significant (see Kleck's metaanalysis in *Point Blank,* pp.
185–215). Kleck believes that the insignificant relationship reflects the
counterbalancing forces stemming from high gun availability: The
bad guys having guns tend to promote crime, but the good guys having guns tend to deter the bad guys.

David McDowall, for one, found no relationship between
gun availability and robbery rates. He had some misgivings about his
findings, however: "[My] results show that the availability of firearms
affects weapons choice in robbery, and that increases in the use of
firearms in robbery stimulates further demand for guns. This leaves
open the possibility that more frequent use of guns in robberies or
higher levels of gun density may have effects on violence other than
those considered here. For example, if gun robberies are more likely
to result in death to the victims than are robberies involving other
weapons [as Cook found], then increases in gun availability may indi-

rectly result in higher homicide rates" (David McDowall, "Gun Availability and Robbery Rates: A Panel Study of Large U.S. Cities, 1974–1978," *Law and Policy* 8 [1986]: 143). See Philip J. Cook, "The Effect of Gun Availability on Robbery and Robbery Murder," in *Policy Studies Review Annual,* ed. Robert Haveman and B. Bruce Zellner (Beverly Hills, Calif.: Sage, 1979), 743–81.

20. *Uniform Crime Reports of the United States, 1993* (Washington, D.C.: Government Printing Office, 1994), 227–28. With baby boomers' children—numbering 40 million—soon to hit their teens, criminologists predict that crime rates will begin rising again by the year 2000; see "Crime Rate Dips Again, But the Future Looks Worse," *New York Times,* November 19, 1995 (as reprinted in *The Providence Sunday Journal,* November 19, 1995, p. A-4).

21. Gene Stephens, "The Global Crime Wave," *The Futurist* (July–August 1994): 23. An interesting national-level experiment on the power of heterogeneity versus tight gun control in explaining high levels of violence is developing in Europe because African, Arab, and Middle East communities are growing rapidly in Belgium, England, France, Germany, and Holland; see Mort Rosenblum, "Culture Clash: Racism, Extremism, and Terrorism Explode in Europe as Immigrants from Africa, Asia, and the Middle East Stream across Borders," Associated Press, reprinted in *The Providence Sunday Journal,* November 19, 1995, pp. D1, D8.

22. Kleck, *Point Blank,* pp. 393–94.

23. See note 4; also see Kleck's review of these and other studies in *Point Blank,* pp. 163–70.

24. See *Uniform Crime Reports, 1993,* pp. 11, 32; Marianne W. Zawitz, *Guns Used in Crime,* Bureau of Justice Statistics Selected Findings, Number 5, NCJ-148201 (Washington, D.C.: U.S. Department of Justice, 1995), 1.

25. See van Dijk, Mayhew, and Killias, *Experiences of Crime across the World: Key Findings from the 1980 International Crime Survey,* 2d ed., p. 37.

26. David Hemenway, "Guns, Public Health, and Public Safety," in *Guns and the Constitution: The Myth of Second Amendment Protection for Firearms in America,* ed. Dennis A. Henigan, E. Bruce Nicholson, and David Hemenway (Northampton, Mass.: Aletheia Press, 1995), 57. However, James D. Wright notes that no one really knows for sure how common or rare heat-of-the-moment homicides really are. "The assumption that they are very common, characteristic

of the pro[gun]control worldview, is derived from the well-known fact that most homicides involve persons known to one another before the event—typically family members, friends, or other acquaintances. But ordinarily, the only people one would ever have any good reason to kill would be people known intimately to oneself. Contrary to the common assumption, prior acquaintance does *not* rule out willful, murderous intent." Wright cites a Kansas City study in which 85 percent of the family homicides followed previous police calls to the family residence to break up domestic quarrels. "It would therefore be misleading to see these homicides as isolated and unfortunate outbursts occurring among normally placid and loving individuals. They are, rather, the culminating episodes of an extended history of violence and abuse among the parties." Finally, he points out that when husbands or boyfriends kill their wives or girlfriends, they usually do it in a "degrading or brutalizing way—such as strangulation or knifing.... [But] firearms equalize the means of physical terror between men and women. In denying the wife of an abusive man the right to have a firearm, we may only be guaranteeing her husband the right to beat her at his pleasure." Thus, one argument against stricter gun control is that "a woman should have as much right to kill her husband as a man has to kill his wife." See Wright, "Second Thoughts about Gun Control."

27. "Suicide Rate Soars among Children, Especially Black Males," *Providence Journal-Bulletin,* April 15, 1995, p. A5 (Associated Press article based on a CDC press release); also see *Sourcebook of Criminal Justice Statistics—1992* (Washington, D.C.: Government Printing Office, 1993), 385, and *Sourcebook of Criminal Justice Statistics—1993* (Washington, D.C.: Government Printing Office, 1994), 391.

David Hemenway's analysis of youth suicide between 1970 and 1990—during which the rate for 15- to 19-year-olds increased 90 percent—brought him to the conclusion that increases were "largely accounted for by the increase in firearm suicides" (see Hemenway, "Guns, Public Health, and Public Safety," p. 55). Don B. Kates and his colleagues caution, however, that suicide among teenagers and young adults has been increasing in much of the industrialized world, even though gun availability is much lower than it is in the United States; see Don B. Kates, Henry E. Schaffer, John K. Lattimer, George B. Murray, and Edwin H. Cassem, "Bad Medicine: Doctors and Guns," in Kopel, *Guns: Who Should Have Them?* p. 257.

28. Firearm death data taken from *Vital Statistics,* published each year by the National Center for Health Statistics of the Public Health Service. For 1993, the most recent year available, firearm deaths totaled 40,240 and were categorized as follows: 18,450 homicides and deaths by legal intervention, 19,590 suicides, 1,740 accidents, and 460 deaths of unknown provenance.

29. See David B. Kopel, "Children and Guns," in Kopel, *Guns: Who Should Have Them?* p. 311.

30. *Statistical Abstract of the United States, 1994* (Washington, D.C.: Government Printing Office, 1994).

31. *Time,* July 17, 1989.

32. Robert J. Mundt, *Canadian Journal of Criminology* 32(1) (January 1990): 144–45.

33. Robert E. Markush and Alfred A. Bartolucci, "Firearms and Suicide in the United States," *American Journal of Public Health* 74 (Fall 1984): 123–27; David Lester, "Availability of Guns and the Likelihood of Suicide," *Sociology and Sociological Research* (July 1987): 287–88; C. Kwing Hung, "Comments on the Article 'Gun Control and Rates of Firearms Violence in Canada and the United States,'" *Canadian Journal of Criminology* 35 (January 1993): 39–40; Robert J. Mundt, "Rejoinder to Comments on 'Gun Control and Rates of Firearms Violence in Canada and the United States,'" *Canadian Journal of Criminology* 35 (January 1993): 45–46; Killias, "International Correlations between Gun Ownership and Rates of Homicide," p. 1723.

34. Kleck, *Point Blank,* pp. 255–68.

35. See Kates, Schaffer, Lattimer, Murray, and Cassem, "Bad Medicine: Doctors and Guns," pp. 255–56. For example, the number of suicides per hundred thousand population for Rumania (66.2), Hungary (39.9), Finland (28.5), Denmark (28.7), France (20.9), Austria (23.6), Switzerland (24.5), Belgium (22.2), West Germany (20.4), Luxembourg (17.8), and Norway (15.6) all exceed that of the United States (12.5).

Chapter Two

1. As quoted in Michael K. Beard and Kristin M. Rand, "Article II," *The Bill of Rights Journal* 20 (December 1987); reprinted in *Gun Control,* ed. Charles P. Cozic and Carol Wekesser (San Diego: Greenhaven Press, 1992), 103–6.

2.   As quoted in Sanford Levinson, "The Embarrassing Second Amendment," *Yale Law Review* 99 (December 1989): 637–59.

3.   John Levin, "The Right to Bear Arms: The Development of the American Experience," *Chicago-Kent Law Review* 48 (Fall–Winter, 1971): 159–62.

4.   For extended excerpts and interpretations of the federal court decisions regarding the Second Amendment, see Earl R. Kruschke, *The Right to Keep and Bear Arms: A Continuing American Dilemma* (Springfield, Ill.: Charles C. Thomas, 1985) and Warren Freedman, *The Privilege to Keep and Bear Arms: The Second Amendment and Its Interpretations* (New York: Quorum Books, 1989).

5.   Glenn Harlan Reynolds, "A Critical Guide to the Second Amendment," *Tennessee Law Review* 62 (Spring 1995): 496.

6.   See Robert J. Cottrol and Raymond T. Diamond, "The Second Amendment: Toward an Afro-Americanist Reconsideration," in *Guns: Who Should Have Them?* ed. David B. Kopel (Amherst, N.Y.: Prometheus, 1995), 127–57. That gun control will hurt minorities and Jews is a favorite topic for discussion in the NRA's monthly magazine *American Rifleman*. See, for example, Elliot C. Rothenberg (former law director of B'nai B'rith's Anti-Defamation League), "Jewish History Refutes Gun Control Activists," *American Rifleman* (February 1988). This contention also provides the ideological foundation for the vehemently anti–gun control group Jews for the Preservation of Firearms Ownership, a tiny ally of the NRA founded by Aaron Zelman in 1989, a self-described gun dealer and gun author. A swastika-headed advertisement for the JPFO reads: "Stop Hitlerism in America! Gun haters who support gun banning, registration, and waiting period schemes are elitist Fascists who want *total* control of people's lives. Gun haters, knowingly or unknowingly, are advocating the Hitler doctrine of the 1990s. Gun control is a tragic mistake of the past. Millions of tortured and mutilated corpses testify to that fact." Finally, gun control as the suppressor of minorities is a common topic on the Internet—see, for example, the talk/politics/guns discussion group on the Usenet.

7.   See, for example, *Firearms Regulations: A Comparative Study of Selected Foreign Nations—Report for Congress #LL94-8* (Washington, D.C.: Library of Congress Law Library, 1994), 66.

8.   "Mississippi Black Code," in *Annals of America* Vol. 9 (Chicago: Encyclopedia Britannica, 1976), 634. This and similar racist gun control laws in the postbellum South are examined in Clayton E.

Cramer, *For the Defense of Themselves and the State: The Original Intent and Judicial Interpretation of the Right to Keep and Bear Arms* (Westport, Conn.: Praeger, 1994), chapter 6. More recent allegations that the purpose of gun regulation is to deprive minorities of firearms are found in Don B. Kates Jr., "Toward a History of Handgun Prohibition," in *Restricting Handguns: The Liberal Skeptics Speak Out* (Great Barrington, Mass.: North River Press, 1979). Kates asserts that the federal and state attempts in the 1960s and 1970s to outlaw Saturday Night Specials were racially motivated. The federal attempt failed—the bill died in committee—while the attempts of several states were successful. *Saturday Night Special* is most likely derived from the phrase "Niggertown Saturday Night," a derogatory characterization of violence among African Americans. Although this etymology is doubted by some, Cramer points out that "the leap from murder as a form of black revelry, to any cheap handgun being a 'niggertown Saturday Night Special,' to the cleaned-up 'Saturday Night Special' is a logical one." Indeed, "if, in fact, the motivations for such laws were racial in nature, we should not be surprised that these statutes were all passed in former slave states" (Cramer, p. 113).

9. For example, Wendy Brown asks the rhetorical question "of what serious assistance are handguns or even machine guns against the arsenal of the modern state?" ("Guns, Cowboys, Philadelphia Mayors, and Civic Republicanism: On Sanford Levinson's *The Embarrassing Second Amendment*," *Yale Law Review* 99 [December 1989]: 661–66.) To this argument the NRA retorts: The claim that a populace equipped only with small arms cannot defeat a modern army is "an unproved theory. The twentieth century provides *no example* of a determined populace with access to small arms having been defeated by a modern army. The Russians lost in Afghanistan, the United States lost in Vietnam, and the French lost in Indo-China. In each case, it was the poorly armed populace that beat the 'modern' army" (Wayne LaPierre, *Guns, Crime, and Freedom,* [Washington, D.C.: Regnery Publishing, 1995], 19–20).

10. See Eric Hirsch, *Urban Revolts: Ethnic Politics in the Nineteenth Century Chicago Labor Movement* (Berkeley and Los Angeles: University of California Press, 1990).

11. Levin, "The Right to Bear Arms: The Development of the American Experience."

12. Robert J. Spitzer, *The Politics of Gun Control* (Chatham, N.J.: Chatham House, 1995), 49.

13. Francis Grose, *Military Antiquities Respecting a History of the English Army* (London, 1812), 1–2; as quoted in David T. Hardy, *Origins and Development of the Second Amendment* (Chino Valley, Ariz.: Blacksmith Publishers, 1986), 13.

14. Grose, pp. 1–2; as quoted in Hardy, p. 14.

15. Hardy, p. 14. For example, England was truly different from France, where between the fifteenth and eighteenth centuries more than 30 different laws were enacted that prevented the population at large from possessing or using arms, especially firearms (see Lee Kennett and James LaVerne Anderson, *The Gun in America: The Origins of a National Dilemma* [Westport, Conn.: Greenwood Press, 1975], 13).

16. 13 Edward I c.1, as quoted in Hardy, p. 15.

17. J. Malcolm, 10 Hast. Con. L.Q., pp. 299–300, as quoted in Hardy, p. 29.

18. As quoted in Hardy, p. 27.

19. "It is necessary for the public safety, that the subjects, which are protestants, should provide and keep arms for their common defense; and that the arms which have been seized and taken from them be restored" (*Journal of the House Commons from Dec. 16, 1688 to Oct. 26, 1693*, p. 17, as quoted in Hardy, pp. 35–36). For a detailed account of the impact of the English civil war on the Anglo-Saxon/American tradition of the right to keep and bear arms, see Joyce Lee Malcolm, *To Keep and Bear Arms: The Origins of an Anglo-American Right* (Cambridge, Mass.: Harvard University Press, 1994).

20. Hardy, p. 41. For a brief historical account of colonial militias as they developed in response to wars with native Americans, see Kennett and Anderson, *The Gun in America,* p. 45. For a detailed account of colonial statutes promoting and regulating militias, see Stephen P. Halbrook, *A Right to Bear Arms: State and Federal Bills of Rights and Constitutional Guarantees* (Westport, Conn.: Greenwood Press, 1989).

21. See H. Treavor Colburn, *The Lamp of Experience: Whig History and the Intellectual Origins of the American Revolution* (Chapel Hill: University of North Carolina Press, 1965). His research involved cataloguing the books in the libraries of Thomas Jefferson, James Madison, Henry Adams, and other framers of the Constitution. Also see Robert E. Shalhope, "The Ideological Origins of the Second Amendment," *Journal of American History* 69 (December 1982): 599–614.

22.   Howard H. Peckman (ed.), *Sources of American Indepen-dence: Selected Manuscripts from the Collection of the William Clements Library,* Vol. 1 (Chicago: University of Chicago Press, 1978), 176.

23.   Stephen P. Halbrook, *A Right to Bear Arms,* p. 17.

24.   For a description of civilian supremacy over the military as debated at the time and eventually framed in the Constitution, see Claude L. Heathcock, *The United States Constitution in Perspective* (Boston: Allyn & Bacon, 1963), 81–82.

25.   Spitzer, *The Politics of Gun Control,* p. 35.

26.   Malcolm, *To Keep and Bear Arms,* p. 161.

27.   Malcolm, *To Keep and Bear Arms,* p. 163. After a detailed analysis of the legislative records of the First Congress and of the indi-vidual state Bill of Rights–ratifying conventions, Clayton E. Cramer arrived at the same conclusion that Malcolm came to after a similarly intensive study of these same records—that is, the framers of the Sec-ond Amendment intended it to protect (a) the right of the states to have militias that could counteract the potential abuses of a standing federal army, and (b) the right of *individuals* to possess ("keep") and carry ("bear") firearms; see Cramer, *For the Defense of Themselves and the State: The Original Intent and Judicial Interpretation of the Right to Keep and Bear Arms,* chapter 3.

28.   As quoted in Malcolm, *To Keep and Bear Arms,* p. 164.

29.   As quoted in Reynolds, "A Critical Guide to the Second Amendment," p. 487.

30.   Shalhope, "The Ideological Origins of the Second Amend-ment."

31.   However, in 42 states *local* governments are preempted from passing their own gun control laws. The NRA, which has fought strongly for preemption laws, argues that they "prevent a hodgepodge of varying gun laws within a state, and thereby protect the law-abiding citizen not only from unwitting violation of the law but also from arbi-trary infringement of his or her rights" (NRA press release, "Why Does Your State Need a Firearms Preemption Law?" 1987). The NRA was prompted into fervent support of preemption laws after Morton Grove (Illinois) passed a local law banning all handguns, a law that was subsequently upheld through appeals all the way to the Supreme Court. Internet users may examine preemption and other state laws via the NRA's Web server: http:/www.nra.org/gun-laws/NRA-FALAWS. html. Users without access to the World Wide Web may use the NRA's ftp (ftp.nra.org/gun-laws/NRA-FALAWS) or gopher (gopher.nra.org/gun-laws/NRA-FALAWS) URLs.

32.   See Edel's discussion of how eighteenth-century conceptions of militias have become anachronistic: Wilbur Edel, *Gun Control: Threat to Liberty or Defense against Anarchy?* (Westport, Conn.: Praeger, 1995), 29–36; see also Brown, "Guns, Cowboys, Philadelphia Mayors, and Civic Republicanism," pp. 661–67.

33.   The 11 states are Hawaii, Maryland, Michigan, Mississippi, New Hampshire, New York, North Carolina, Oregon, Pennsylvania, South Carolina, and Washington.

34.   Spitzer, *The Politics of Gun Control,* p. 49.

35.   As quoted in Lawrence Delbert Cress, "An Armed Community: The Origins and Meaning of the Right to Bear Arms," *Journal of American History* 71 (June 1984): 42. For a descriptive cataloguing of the dozens of state and federal court decisions interpreting the Second Amendment as protecting the right of states to form militias and *not* the right of individuals to keep and bear arms, see Freedman, *The Privilege to Keep and Bear Arms: The Second Amendment and Its Interpretations,* chapter 2.

36.   Congress created the National Guard in 1903 and put it under close federal control with the National Defense Act of 1916. As private militia-movement groups increasingly come face to face with the law, we can expect to see more court rulings on what constitutes the *militia* described in the Second Amendment. According to legal historian Glenn Harlan Reynolds, private militia groups that argue *they* are the militia that the Constitution describes have it wrong: "Although the militia was a body that was, in a way, external to the state in the sense of being an institution of the people, the expectation was that the state, not private groups, would provide the foundation upon which the structure of the militia would be erected" (Reynolds, "A Critical Guide to the Second Amendment," p. 509). Private militias have received considerable press since militia members were implicated in the bombing of the Alfred P. Murrah Federal Building in Oklahoma City that took 167 lives in April 1995. See, for example, "The Fight to Bear Arms," *U.S. News and World Report* (May 22, 1995), p. 28–37; and "Up In Arms about a Revolting Movement," *Chicago Tribune,* January 30, 1995, p. 11.

Chapter Three

1.   Richard Maxwell Brown, "Historical Patterns of Violence," in *Violence in America,* Vol. II, ed. Ted Robert Gurr (Newbury Park, Calif.: Sage, 1989) 23, 48.

2. David B. Kopel, *The Samurai, the Mountie, and the Cowboy: Should America Adopt the Gun Controls of Other Democracies?* (Buffalo, N.Y.: Prometheus, 1992), 311.

3. Among others, Lee Kennett and James LaVerne Anderson, *The Gun in America: The Origins of a National Dilemma* (Westport, Conn.: Greenwood Press, 1975), 145.

4. Don B. Kates Jr., "Comparisons among Nations and over Time," in *The Gun Control Debate: You Decide,* ed. Lee Nisbet (Buffalo, N.Y.: Prometheus Books, 1990), 189–90. In the view of some, Europe has evolved socially to a higher plane. Bruce-Briggs describes this view (not his own) as follows: "Bourgeois Europe [is] a model of a civilized society: A society just, equitable, and democratic; but well ordered, with the lines of responsibility and authority clearly drawn, and ... [where] personal violence is shameful, and uncontrolled gun ownership a blot on civilization" (B. Bruce-Briggs, "The Great American Gun War," *Public Interest* 45 (Fall 1976): 61.

5. See Brown, "Historical Patterns of Violence," for an overview of these topics.

6. Jay Miller, "Blending Two Worlds," in *The Native Americans* (Atlanta: Turner Publishing, 1993), 186.

7. See Miller, "Blending Two Worlds," p. 189.

8. Bob Wyss, "A Massacre Incited by Racial Hatred," *The Providence Sunday Journal,* December 31, 1995, pp. A-1, A-16.

9. See Miller, "Blending Two Worlds," p. 191; Richard Hofstadter and Michael Wallace, "America as a Gun Culture," *American Heritage* 21 (October 1970): 7–8; John A. Garraty, *The American Nation: A History of the United States to 1877,* 2d ed. (New York: Harper and Row, 1971), 21.

10. Wyss, "A Massacre Incited by Racial Hatred," p. A-16. Even Rhode Island's founder, Roger Williams, though his relationship with local Indians was so cordial that they spared his life once when they attacked and destroyed much of Providence, called local natives "barbarous scum and offsourings of mankinde" (see Wyss, p. A-16).

11. Richard White, "Expansion and Exodus," in *The Native Americans,* pp. 263–81; see also Garraty, *The American Nation,* p. 95.

12. Garraty, *The American Nation,* p. 93.

13. Garraty, *The American Nation,* p. 67.

14. Hofstadter and Wallace, "America as a Gun Culture," p. 10.

15. Hofstadter and Wallace, "America as a Gun Culture," p. 10.

16. White, "Expansion and Exodus," p. 292.

17. Peter Nabokov, "Long Threads," in *The Native Americans,* pp. 322–77.

18. W. Eugene Hollon, *Frontier Violence: Another Look* (New York: Oxford University Press, 1974), 57.

19. Hollon, p. 62.

20. Brown, "Historical Patterns of Violence," p. 40.

21. See Kennett and Anderson, *The Gun in America,* pp. 15–126. Also see Richard Slotkin, *Gunfighter Nation: The Myth of the Frontier in Twentieth-Century America* (New York: Atheneum, 1992), chapters 2–6.

22. "The Rifle," *Buffalo Bill's Wild West* program, 1886, 1893, as quoted in Slotkin, *Gunfighter Nation,* p. 77.

23. Garraty, *The American Nation,* p. 83.

24. Kennett and Anderson, *The Gun in America,* p. 48.

25. Garraty, *The American Nation,* p. 93.

26. Quoted in Theodore M. Hammett, "Two Mobs of Jacksonian Boston: Ideology and Interest," *Journal of American History* 62 (March 1976): 860.

27. David R. Goldfield and Blaine A. Brownell, *Urban America: A History* (Boston: Houghton Mifflin, 1990), 158.

28. Roger Lane, "Urbanization and Criminal Violence in the Nineteenth Century," *Journal of American History* 2 (December 1968): 156; see also Ted Robert Gurr, "Historical Trends in Violent Crime: Europe and the United States," in *Violence in America,* Vol. I, ed. Ted Robert Gurr (Newbury Park, Calif.: Sage, 1989), 21–51.

29. Goldfield and Brownell, *Urban America,* pp. 158–61; also see Richard Hofstadter and Michael Wallace (eds.), *American Violence: A Documentary History* (New York: Knopf, 1970). Of course, in the South, group violence was common against African Americans. Ku Klux Klan members and less formally organized white mobs were involved in 80 riots against freed slaves in the first decade after the Civil War. White supremacy was reinforced by lynching. At its peak between 1891 and 1901, more than 100 victims a year were hung; overall, between 1882 and 1951, 3,400 African Americans lost their lives to lynching. (See Ted Robert Gurr, "The History of Protest, Rebellion, and Reform in America: An Overview," in Gurr, *Violence in America,* Vol. I, p. 11.)

30. However, in many riots of the era, unarmed mobs would arm themselves by looting gun stores; see Hofstadter and Wallace, *American Violence,* p. 26, and Kennett and Anderson, *The Gun in America,* p. 146.

31. Lane, "Urbanization and Criminal Violence in the Nineteenth Century."

32. William A. Gamson, *The Strategy of Social Protest*, 2d ed. (Belmont, Calif.: Wadsworth, 1990), 82.

33. See Philip J. Ethington, "Vigilantes and Police: The Creation of a Professional Police Bureaucracy in San Francisco, 1847–1900," *Journal of Social History* 21 (Winter 1987): 197–227; Robert M. Fogelson, *Big-City Police* (Cambridge, Mass.: Harvard University Press, 1977); Sidney L. Harring, *Policing a Class Society: The Experience of American Cities, 1865 to 1915* (New Brunswick, N.J.: Rutgers University Press, 1983); Roger Lane, *Policing the City: Boston, 1822–1885* (Cambridge, Mass.: Harvard University Press, 1967); and Eric H. Monkkonen, *Police in Urban America, 1860–1920* (New York: Cambridge University Press, 1981).

34. Gurr, "The History of Violent Crime in America," p. 37; see also Roger Lane, *Violent Death in the City: Suicide, Accident, and Murder in Nineteenth-Century Philadelphia* (Cambridge, Mass.: Harvard University Press, 1979).

35. See Brown, "Historical Patterns of Violence."

36. See Brown, "Historical Patterns of Violence," pp. 37–39; see also Richard Maxwell Brown, *Strain of Violence: Historical Studies of American Violence and Vigilantism* (New York: Oxford University Press, 1975).

37. Richard Maxwell Brown, "The American Vigilante Tradition," in *Violence in America: Historical and Comparative Perspectives,* ed. Hugh Graham Davis and Ted Robert Gurr (Washington, D.C.: Government Printing Office, 1969), 152.

38. Hollon, *Frontier Violence,* p. 211.

39. Roger D. McGrath, "Violence and Lawlessness on the Western Frontier," pp. 122–45 in Gurr, *Violence in America,* Vol. I.

40. See Hollon, *Frontier Violence,* chapter 10.

41. *Laws of Indiana, 1831,* as quoted in Clayton E. Cramer, *For the Defense of Themselves and the State: The Original Intent and Judicial Interpretation of the Right to Keep and Bear Arms* (Westport, Conn.: Praeger, 1994), 72.

42. Wilbur Edel, *Gun Control: Threat to Liberty or Defense against Anarchy?* (Westport, Conn.: Praeger, 1995), chapter 4; also see Kennett and Anderson, *The Gun in America,* p. 159.

43. *The State v. Reid,* I Ala. 1612, cited in Kennett and Anderson, *The Gun in America,* p. 161. See chapter 2 for other court deci-

sions supporting the right of local, state, and federal government to infringe upon the right of an individual to keep and bear arms.

44. Billington, *America's Frontier Heritage,* pp. 73, 94.

45. Hollon, *Frontier Violence,* p. x.

46. Hofstadter and Wallace, *American Violence,* pp. 11–12.

Chapter Four

1. James A. Davis and Tom W. Smith, *General Social Surveys, 1972–1994* (Chicago: National Opinion Research Center, 1995). Distributed by Roper Public Opinion Research Center, Storrs, Conn.

2. *Proposed Comprehensive Bill of Handgun Control, Inc.* (Washington, D.C.: Handgun Control Inc., 1995), 2.

3. *Ten Myths about Gun Control* (Fairfax, Va.: National Rifle Association Institute for Legislative Action, 1994), 2.

4. Gary Kleck, "Bad Data and the 'Evil Empire': Interpreting Poll Data on Gun Control," *Violence and Victims* 8 (Winter 1993): 374.

5. For a review of the findings of many of these polls through the late 1970s, see Tom W. Smith, "The 75% Solution: An Analysis of the Structure of Attitudes on Gun Control, 1959–1977," *Journal of Criminal Law and Criminology* 71 (1980): 300–316, and James D. Wright, "Public Opinion and Gun Control," *Annals of the American Academy of Political and Social Science* 453 (May 1981): 24–39; for a similar review through 1990, see Gary Kleck, *Point Blank: Guns and Violence in America* (New York: Aldine de Gruyter, 1991), 378–83. Since 1990, key polls have included those done by Harris (Elizabeth Hann Hastings and Philip K. Hastings [eds.], *Index to International Public Opinion, 1990–1991* [Westport, Conn.: Greenwood Press, 1992], 356); Gallup (David W. Moore and Frank Newport, "Public Strongly Favors Stricter Gun Control Laws," *The Gallup Poll Monthly* [January 1994]: 18–24); *USA Today* and CNN (Dennis Cauchon, "Poll: Owners Favor Gun Laws," *USA Today,* March 17, 1993, p. 1); the *Washington Post* and ABC News ("Poll Says Crime Becoming Top Public Concern," *Washington Post,* as reprinted in the *Providence Journal-Bulletin,* November 16, 1993, p. A-3); and the *New York Times* and CBS (Elizabeth Hann Hastings and Philip K. Hastings [eds.], *Index to International Public Opinion, 1992–1993* [Westport, Conn.: Greenwood Press, 1994], 493).

6. For intensive analysis of the effects of wording gun control questions on surveys, see Howard Schuman and Stanley Presser,

"Attitude Measurement and the Gun Control Paradox," *Public Opinion Quarterly* 41 (1977–1978): 427–38; they conclude that "regardless of [question] form, a clear majority of the public favors GR [gun registration]" (p. 431).

7. See James A. Davis and Tom W. Smith, *The NORC General Social Survey: A User's Guide* (Newbury Park, Calif.: Sage, 1992). The GSS was not conducted in 1979, 1981, or 1992. Since 1994, the GSS has been conducted biannually (1994, 1996) on a sample of approximately 3,000 individuals.

8. See *Proposed Comprehensive Bill of Handgun Control, Inc.* (Washington, D.C.: Handgun Control Inc., 1995), 1–7.

9. Kleck, *Point Blank,* p. 375.

10. As quoted in Ted Gest, "Battle over Gun Control Heats Up across the U.S.," *U.S. News and World Report* (May 31, 1982): 38.

11. See Kleck, *Point Blank,* pp. 3–7.

12. For example, the relationship between conservatism and gun ownership in the cumulated 1991–1994 General Social Surveys is as follows:

		Gun Owner		
		No	Yes	(Row Sum)
	Liberal	65.9% (716)	34.1% (370)	100% (1,086)
Political Views	Moderate	58.3% (842)	41.7% (603)	100% (1,445)
	Conservative	52.6% (700)	47.4% (632)	100% (1,332)
(Column Sum)		(2,258)	(1,605)	$N = 3,863$

Note: Percentages are calculated by row and should therefore be compared by column. Thus, as political views move from liberal to conservative, we find a (47.4 − 34.1 =) 13.4 percent greater chance of an individual being a gun owner.

13. According to Kleck, "liberalism and support for gun control have become closely linked in the public mind. Surveys have documented a rough association between gun control support and a wide variety of other opinions conventionally associated with liberalism. Interestingly, it turns out that this link is solely due to higher gun own-

ership among conservatives—gun-owning liberals are no more likely to support gun control than gun-owning conservatives" (*Point Blank,* pp. 6–7). However, the following tables, calculated from the cumulated 1991–1994 General Social Surveys, show that Kleck overstates his case.

Require a Police Permit to Buy a Gun?

		Oppose	Favor	(Row Sum)
	Liberal	13.0% (140)	87.0% (940)	100% (1,080)
Political Views	Moderate	18.4% (264)	81.6% (1,173)	100% (1,437)
	Conservative	24.6% (327)	75.4% (1,004)	100% (1,331)
(Column Sum)		(731)	(3,117)	$N = 3,848$

(All Respondents)

Require a Police Permit to Buy a Gun?

		Oppose	Favor	(Row Sum)
	Liberal	7.5% (53)	92.5% (653)	100% (706)
Political Views	Moderate	10.3% (86)	89.7% (746)	100% (832)
	Conservative	14.9% (103)	85.1% (586)	100% (689)
(Column Sum)		(242)	(1,985)	$N = 2,227$

(Non–Gun Owners Only)

Require a Police Permit
to Buy a Gun?

		Oppose	Favor	(Row Sum)
	Liberal	22.8% (84)	77.2% (285)	100% (369)
Political Views	Moderate	29.4% (174)	70.6% (417)	100% (591)
	Conservative	34.1% (213)	65.9% (411)	100% (624)
(Column Sum)		(471)	(1,113)	$N = 1,584$

(Gun Owners Only)

Note: Percentages are calculated by row and should therefore be compared by column. Thus, in the first table, as political views move from liberal to conservative, we find a (87.0 − 75.4 =) 11.6 percent smaller chance of an individual favoring the idea that a police permit should be required to buy a gun. This relationship maintains itself in both partial tables, though it does weaken to a 7.4 percent difference for non–gun owners only. If Kleck were correct, the percentage difference between liberal and conservative would have approached zero in both partial tables.

14. Erich Goode, *Sociology* (Englewood Cliffs, N.J.: Prentice-Hall, 1984), 230.

15. Goode, *Sociology,* p. 321.

16. The lack of significant relationships between attitudes on gun control and social class or age has been consistent across time. Smith's analyses of Harris, NORC, and University of Michigan survey data collected in the 1950s, 1960s, and 1970s led him to conclude that there is "no relationship between age and gun control over the period," and, moreover, that the "stratification variables [of] education and income ... show no relationship to attitudes on gun control ... which has not changed over time" (see Smith, "The 75% Solution," pp. 302–4).

Note that the slight relationships in table 4.1 that do exist between support for gun control and social class or age are positive. This bodes well for advocates of gun control, because voting is strongly positively related to both social class (as measured by income, occupational prestige, and education) and age. See Leonard Beeghley, "Social

Class and Political Participation," *Sociological Forum* (1 Summer 1986): 496–513; Gregg Lee Carter, *Solutions Manual for Analyzing Contemporary Social Issues* (Boston: Allyn & Bacon, 1996), 41–47; and Vincent N. Parrillo, John Stimson, and Ardyth Stimson, *Contemporary Social Problems,* 2d ed. (Boston: Allyn & Bacon, 1990), 417.

17.   See Edward Diener and Kenneth W. Kerber, "Personality Characteristics and American Gun Owners," *Journal of Social Psychology* (Spring 1979): 227–38; Jo Dixon and Alan J. Lizotte, "Gun Ownership and the 'Southern Subculture of Violence,' " *American Journal of Sociology* 93 (September 1987): 383–405; Gary D. Hill, Frank M. Howell, and Ernest T. Driver, "Gender, Fear, and Protective Handgun Ownership," *Criminology* 23 (August 1985): 541–52; Alan J. Lizotte and David J. Bordua, "Firearms Ownership for Sport and Protection: Two Divergent Models," *American Sociological Review* 45 (April 1980): 229–44; Kleck, *Point Blank,* especially pp. 372–84; Paula D. McClain, "Firearms Ownership, Gun Control Attitudes, and Neighborhood Environment," *Law and Policy Quarterly* 5 (1983): 299–323; Smith, "The 75% Solution"; Tom R. Tyler and Paul J. Lavrakas, "Support for Gun Control: The Influence of Personal, Sociotropic, and Ideological Concerns," *Journal of Applied Social Psychology* 13 (Spring 1983): 392–405; J. Sherwood Williams, J. Marolla, and John H. McGrath, "Firearms and Urban American Women," in *Comparing Female and Male Offenders,* ed. M. Q. Warren (Beverly Hills, Calif.: Sage, 1981), 106–22; and Robert L. Young, "The Protestant Heritage and the Spirit of Gun Ownership," *Journal for the Scientific Study of Religion* 28 (September 1989): 300–309.

18.   The logit parameter estimates for the dependent variable gun law (0 = oppose; 1 = favor) are provided below.

Independent Variable	Coefficient	Standard Error	Significance	Odds Ratio
Owns Gun	−0.709	0.109	<0.001	0.492
Hunter	−1.103	0.124	<0.001	0.332
Conservatism	−0.308	0.063	<0.001	0.735
Urbanization	0.081	0.053	<0.007	1.084
Gender	0.469	0.106	<0.001	1.598

(0 = male; 1 = female)

Chi-square = 356.4 (df = 5; sig. =.001)

−2 Log likelihood = 2694.1

Although the dependent variable is binary, Kleck argues that ordinary least-squares (OLS) regression analysis "is an acceptable estimation procedure because the split on the item [78 percent in favor, 22 percent opposed] is not an extreme one" (*Point Blank,* p. 373). OLS regression estimates are displayed below (note: all coefficients are significant at the .01 level, except for urbanization):

Independent Variable	Unstandardized Coefficient	Standard Error	Standardized Coefficient	t-value
Owns Gun	−0.098	0.015	−0.122	−6.5
Hunter	−0.238	0.021	−0.221	−11.5
Conservatism	−0.041	0.008	−0.084	−5.0
Urbanization	0.011	0.007	0.026	1.5
Gender	0.061	0.014	0.078	4.3

(0 = male; 1 = female)

F = 89.7 (N = 3,137; sig. =.001)

$R^2 = 0.125$

19.   The following observations are provided for those readers not accustomed to reading diagrams such as that in figure 4.4. The plus (+) and the minus (−) signs denote how each pair of variables is related. For example, the minus sign between urban and hunter means that urban dwellers are less likely to be hunters than their counterparts (country dwellers). Similarly, the plus sign between gender (male) and hunter means that men are more likely to be hunters than their counterparts (women). (And so on for the other diagrammed relationships.)

20.   *Ten Myths about Gun Control,* p. 2.

21.   *Ten Myths about Gun Control,* p. 3. An example of a locality voting down a proposed gun control regulation is Madison, Wisconsin, where in 1993 voters rejected a proposal to ban handgun ownership in the city.

22.   Kleck, *Point Blank,* pp. 365–66.

23.   Howard Schuman and Stanley Presser, "The Attitude-Action Connection and the Issue of Gun Control," *Annals of the American Academy of Political and Social Science* 455 (May 1981): 40–47. Also see their analysis of the 1976 GSS item "compared to how you feel on other public issues, are your feelings on [gun control] extremely strong, fairly strong, or not very strong"; the overwhelming majority of

both pro– (90 percent) and anti– (82 percent) gun control respondents answered either fairly or extremely strong. Analysis of these and other data led Schuman and Presser to conclude that "we have not been able to show that gun registration opponents actually outnumber proponents among those most intensely involved in the issue and, in fact, our data show overall intensity is greater among proponents" (p. 437).

24. Schuman and Presser, "The Attitude-Action Connection and the Issue of Gun Control."

25. Schuman and Presser, "The Attitude-Action Connection and the Issue of Gun Control," p. 46.

26. Kleck writes that "in 1978, when these data were gathered, less than 1% of the population were NRA members. At most perhaps 10 of the 1070 persons in Schuman and Presser's sample were NRA members. Even if all of these 10 were among the 85 opponents who reported taking actions (writing letters, etc.), that would still have left at least 75 non-NRA opponents reporting actions, i.e., 18.0% of all opponents, vs. only 7.1% among supporters. Even among people not subject to the NRA's mobilization efforts, opponents were far more likely to have acted on their beliefs than were supporters" (*Point Blank,* p. 365).

27. *Ten Myths about Gun Control,* p. 2.

28. *Time,* May 10, 1994, p. 16.

29. *Providence Journal-Bulletin,* December 6, 1995, p. A-14.

Chapter Five

1. Leroy N. Rieselbach, *Congressional Politics: The Evolving Legislative System,* 2d ed. (Boulder, Colo.: Westview Press, 1995), 5.

2. Pete Shields, *Guns Don't Die—People Do* (New York: Arbor House, 1981), 93–94.

3. Edward F. Leddy, *Magnum Force: The National Rifle Association Fights Gun Control* (New York: University Press of America, 1987), 1.

4. Osha Gray Davidson, *Under Fire: The NRA and the Battle for Gun Control* (New York: Henry Holt and Company, 1993), 145–46.

5. As quoted in Ted Gest, "Battle over Gun Control Heats Up across the U.S.," *U.S. News and World Report* (May 31, 1982): 35–36.

6. As quoted in Robert Sherrill, *The Saturday Night Special* (New York: Charterhouse, 1973), 201.

7. For example, McAdam, McCarthy, and Zald maintain that "the real action in social movements takes place at some level inter-

mediate between the macro and micro. It is there in the existing asso-
ciational groups or networks of the aggrieved community that the first
groping steps toward collective action are taken. It is there that the
decision to embed the movement in more formal movement organizations is reached. And it is there within the SMOs [social-movement
organizations] themselves, that the strategic decisions are made that
shape the trajectory of the movement over time.... The intermediate
meso level ... is *the* level at which most movement action occurs" (p.
729). See Doug McAdam, John D. McCarthy, and Mayer N. Zald,
"Social Movements," in *Handbook of Sociology,* ed. Neil J. Smelser
(Newbury Park, Calif.: Sage, 1988), 695–737.

8.   See Davidson, *Under Fire,* chapter 2, and Mark A. Keefe,
"NRA, Celebrating 125 Years of Service to America," *American Rifleman* (January 1996): 40–45.

9.   As quoted in Carol Skalnik Leff and Mark H. Leff, "The
Politics of Ineffectiveness: Federal Firearms Legislation, 1919–1938,"
Annals of the American Academy of Political and Social Science 455
(May 1981): 53.

10.   Leff and Leff, "The Politics of Ineffectiveness," p. 55.

11.   Leff and Leff, "The Politics of Ineffectiveness," p. 55.

12.   Leff and Leff, "The Politics of Ineffectiveness," p. 55.

13.   Leff and Leff, "The Politics of Ineffectiveness," pp. 60, 62.

14.   Davidson, *Under Fire,* p. 28.

15.   As quoted in Davidson, *Under Fire,* p. 30.

16.   "Are We Really So Violent?" *American Rifleman* (March
1968): 16.

17.   "Restraint on ... Cheap Handguns Wins Favor," *American
Rifleman* (March 1968): 16.

18.   *Senate Hearings on Saturday Night Special Ban,* Septem-
ber 13, 1971, pp. 315, 323; as quoted in Josh Sugarmann, *National
Rifle Association: Money, Firepower, Fear* (Washington, D.C.: National
Press Books, 1992), 42.

19.   See Sherrill, *The Saturday Night Special,* p. 193.

20.   As quoted in Sugarmann, *NRA: Money, Firepower, Fear,* p. 48.

21.   As quoted in Shields, *Guns Don't Die—People Do,* p. 22,
and reaffirmed in a personal interview.

22.   The history of Handgun Control Incorporated has been
cobbled together from interviews with three of the organization's
original founders, Mark Borinsky, Jeanne Shields (Pete Shields's
spouse), and Edward Welles; Pete Shields's *Guns Don't Die—People*

Do; Sugarmann's *National Rifle Association: Money, Firepower, Fear,* especially pp. 253–59; interviews with current HCI officials, as well as various flyers distributed by HCI, including "Handgun Control Inc. at a Glimpse," (Washington, D.C.: Handgun Control Inc., 1995); and Sashai A. McClure, "An Analysis of Handgun Control, Inc." (Castro Valley, Calif.: Combat Arms, 1995), as posted on the UseNet's talk.politics.guns on April 18, 1995. The Shields book is particularly important; as one of the founders of HCI, he is able to give a detailed account of the early days of the organization. On the other hand, the McClure document contains errors and should be relied on only when confirmed by other sources. HCI administrators created a sister organization in 1983, the Center to Prevent Handgun Violence (CPHV), to handle its education and media-relations duties; CPHV was also created to encourage contributions to the gun control cause, since donations and membership dues are tax deductible—unlike moneys given to HCI (because of HCI's involvement in lobbying). Although CPHV is legally a separate corporate entity, it shares offices and many staff members with HCI and will be considered simply as one of HCI's several major organizational divisions for the purposes of this chapter.

23.   Definitions and examples for the constructs from figures 5.1 to 5.3 rely heavily on McAdam, McCarthy, and Zald, "Social Movements." Figure 5.1 also draws on Hanspeter Kriesi, Ruud Koopmans, Jan Weillem Duyvendak, and Marco G. Giugni, *New Social Movements in Western Europe: A Comparative Analysis* (Minneapolis: University of Minnesota Press, 1995).

24.   Snow and Benford would call this *zeitgeist* a "master frame" around which most of the movements of the era were organized. *Frames* are interpretative schemes that simplify the "world out there" and help individuals to organize their thinking and actions. The general frame used repeatedly by the activists of the 1960s was that a particular social fact or social arrangement was unjust, and further that it was unnecessary because collective action against the right targets (e.g., government, corporations) could rectify the situation. See David A. Snow and Robert D. Benford, "Master Frames and Cycles of Protest," in *Frontiers in Social Movement Theory,* ed. Aldon D. Morris and Carol McClurg Mueller (New Haven, Conn.: Yale University Press, 1992), 133–55.

25.   By the 1980s, there were 20,000 registered and unregistered lobbyists in Washington, D.C., and lobbying had become "the

fourth largest business in the nation's capital, after government, printing, and tourism." Louis Rukeyser and John Cooney, *Louis Rukeyser's Business Almanac* (New York: Simon and Schuster, 1991), 141.

26. BATF's attempt to set up gun records was aborted when the 1978 Treasury Appropriations Subcommittee cut $4.2 million (the estimated first-year cost) from BATF's budget with the following prohibition: "No funds appropriated herein shall be available for salaries or administrative expense in connection with consolidating or centralizing, within the Department of the Treasury, the records, or any portion thereof, of acquisition and disposition of firearms maintained by Federal firearms licensees." This prohibition was later incorporated into the 1986 Firearms Owners' Protection Act. See "Noncombatants Guide to the Gun Control Fight," *Changing Times* (August 1979): 33–36; Neal Knox, "Knox's Notebook: BATF Again Registering Guns," *American Rifleman* (April 1995): 14.

27. As quoted in Gest, "Battle over Gun Control Heats Up across the U.S.," p. 37. The NRA pulls out this epithet from time to time, most recently in its characterization of several well-publicized BATF raids in the early 1990s that went awry, including the assault on David Koresh and his Branch Davidians sect that left 80 Branch Davidians and four federal agents dead. See Sue Anne Pressly, "House Opens Hearings into Fatal Siege," *Washington Post,* as reprinted in the *Providence Journal-Bulletin,* July 20, 1995, pp. A-1, A-10. Another favorite epithet is "armed terrorists" (see "Time for Congress to Rein in BATF," *American Rifleman* [April 1995]: 39). When the NRA's Executive Vice President Wayne LaPierre used the epithet "jack-booted thugs" in the spring of 1995, George Bush promptly sent the NRA his resignation in the form of a letter castigating LaPierre. LaPierre later apologized, emphasizing that he did not mean that all federal law enforcement officials were "jack-booted thugs," only a few BATF agents; see Liane Hansen and Daniel Schorr, "Oklahoma City Disaster Prompts National Mood Change," *National Public Radio Weekend Edition,* May 21, 1995 (transcript #1124–10).

28. CDC has the habit of editorializing the data it releases to the public in a manner that pleases HCI and infuriates the NRA. For example, the August 1994 release of firearms injury data was accompanied by the following statement from CDC's director, Dr. David Satcher: "We are destroying our future with firearms. It's not just lives lost, but lives injured or maimed ... children who are too afraid to play in the streets" (see A. J. Hostetler, "Guns Cost One Million Life-Years

CDC Says," *Providence Journal-Bulletin,* August 26, 1994, p. A-12). These comments were similar to those Satcher had made several months before: "Anything we can do to get guns out of the hands of children and out of homes would reduce the fatality rate. They may still fight, but they'll do it like we did, with fists and maybe rocks. Not with guns" (see Jean Latz Griffin and William Recktenwald, "Sentiment Grows for Gun Curb Legislation," *Chicago Tribune,* as reprinted in the *Providence Journal-Bulletin,* November 4, 1993, p. 1). Defunding BATF and CDC is a favorite topic on the NRA listservs (e.g., alerts@NRA.org) and Gun-Talk bulletin board (703–934–2121); also see "CDC under Fire," *NRA Grass Fire* 1 (December 1995): 1–2. *NRA Grass Fire* is published by the NRA's Institute for Legislative Action and is available on its NRA listservs and home page (http://www.nra.org/pub/ila/).

29. Aldon D. Morris, *The Origins of the Civil Rights Movement: Black Communities Organizing for Change* (New York: Free Press, 1984).

30. Personal interview with Jeanne Shields. There is no real institutional memory within the current staff of HCI. Pete Shields is deceased, Mark Borinsky has moved on to a career in the private sector, and Edward Welles maintains only brief and occasional contact with the organization he helped to found.

31. See Shields, *Guns Don't Die—People Do,* p. 103.

32. Quoted statements were made by Pete Shields, the founding chair of HCI; see Sugarmann, *National Rifle Association: Money, Power, Fear,* p. 257.

33. See Shields, *Guns Don't Die—People Do,* p. 97.

34. Sherrill, *The Saturday Night Special,* p. 196.

35. Shields, *Guns Don't Die—People Do,* p. 105.

36. This and subsequent quotes in this paragraph are taken from Joseph Tataro, *Revolt at Cincinnati* (Buffalo: Hawkeye Publishing, 1981), 5–22, as quoted in Sugarmann, *NRA: Money, Firepower, Fear,* chapter 2.

37. Carter's argument for keeping derringers legal so that children could defend themselves anticipates NRA Executive Director Tanya Metaksa's argument 24 years later that the easy-grip feature of assault rifles makes them the weapon of choice for many handicapped people, and this is one reason why the 1994 legislation banning 19 kinds of assault rifles needs to be repealed. See January 18, 1996, video of CBS's *This Morning* show.

38. As an "oldtime NRA moderate" wrote in a letter to another NRA moderate, Robert Sherrill; see his *The Saturday Night Special,* pp. 185–86.

39. Sherrill, *The Saturday Night Special,* p. 186.

40. As quoted in Sherrill, *The Saturday Night Special,* p. 188.

41. Davidson, *Under Fire,* p. 35. The account of the Cincinnati Revolt presented here relies heavily on Davidson's book, as well as on Tartaro, *Revolt at Cincinnati*; Sugarmann, *NRA: Money, Firepower, Fear,* chapter 2; and Leddy, *Magnum Force Lobby,* chapter 6.

42. As reported in Wayne LaPierre, "Standing Guard," *American Rifleman* (October 1995): 7.

43. LaPierre, "Standing Guard," p. 7.

44. As quoted in Davidson, *Under Fire,* p. 38.

45. As quoted in Davidson, *Under Fire,* pp. 38–39.

46. Charles J. Orasin, "Handgun Control and the Politics of Fear," *USA Today,* January 1980, pp. 8–10.

47. See Theda Skocpol, *States and Social Revolutions* (New York: Cambridge University Press, 1979).

48. Robert Reinhold, "After Shooting, Horror but Few Answers," *New York Times,* January 19, 1989, p. B-6.

49. Charles Mohr, "U.S. Bans Imports of Assault Rifles in Shift by Bush," *New York Times,* February 17, 1989, p. 1.

50. The political dealings and machinations Clinton used are detailed nicely in Robert J. Spitzer, *The Politics of Gun Control* (Chatham, N.J.: Chatham House, 1995), 153–57.

51. "NRA Showed It Still Had What It Takes to Overcome Gun-Control Advocates," *CQ Almanac, 1988* (Washington, D.C.: Congressional Quarterly, 1989), 100–101.

52. Wayne La Pierre, *Guns, Crime, and Freedom* (Washington, D.C.: Regnery Publishing, 1994), 83–84.

53. As quoted in Spitzer, *The Politics of Gun Control,* p. 162. Also see Steven A. Holmes, "Rifle Lobby Torn by Dissidents and Capitol Defectors," *New York Times,* March 27, 1991, p. 1.

54. See *Brady II: The Gun Violence Prevention Act of 1994* (Washington, D.C.: Handgun Control Inc., 1994); "Proposed Comprehensive Bill of Handgun Control, Inc.," (Washington, D.C.: Handgun Control Inc., 1995); and Richard L. Worsnop, "Gun Control," *CQ Researcher* 4 (June 10, 1994): 522–23. For a description of the 1995 version of Brady II (almost identical to the 1994 version), H.R. 1321 and S. 631, see Keith Bea, *CRS Issue Brief: Gun Control,* (Washington,

D.C.: Library of Congress Congressional Research Service, September 8, 1995; order code IB94007), 8–9.

55. For an analysis of the NRA's campaign strategy in the 1994 elections, see the videotape of CNN's *Crossfire,* November 1, 1994.

56. Neal Knox, "Knox's Notebook: Congress Changed; Gun-Laws Maybe," *American Hunter* (January/February 1995): 10; "Protecting Freedom '95," *American Rifleman* (June 1995): 48–51.

57. Cited in Neal Knox, "Republicans Promise to Support NRA," *Guns and Ammo* (May 1995): 16.

58. For a thorough description of congressional committees and their pivotal role in the legislative process, see Rieselbach, *Congressional Politics,* especially chapters 4 and 11.

59. As quoted in Knox, "Republicans Promise to Support NRA," p. 16.

60. Neal Knox, "From the Capitol: Anti-Gun Lawmakers Go Down in Flames," *Guns and Ammo* (February 1995): 22.

61. See Worsnop, "Gun Control," p. 522, and "Brady Bill Triggers Suit by Sheriff," *Providence Journal-Bulletin,* February 24, 1994, p. A-4. The first such ruling came from U.S. District Judge Charles Lovell of Helena, Montana: "The Congress does not have the power to force local law enforcement, particularly the local sheriff, to carry out the federal government's mandates." Lovell ruled that, in effect, the Brady law violated the Tenth Amendment, which circumscribes federal authority over state interests. Gun control proponents are challenging these rulings, but both sides of the debate feel that the issue will be moot by the time it reaches the Supreme Court. The Brady law provided funding for the states to computerize their records within five years so that instant checks could be done and background checks by local authorities will become unnecessary. As of January 1996, 12 states had already instituted instant checks.

62. All researchers and others with serious interest in current federal legislation can use the Internet to keep themselves informed. The Thomas home page of the Library of Congress provides all of this information, is easy to use, and is updated almost daily: http://thomas.loc.gov/. The NRA's interpretation of current gun control legislation can be found using their Institute for Legislative Action's home page: http://www.nra.org.

63. For example, see Liane Hansen and Daniel Schorr, "Oklahoma City Disaster Prompts National Mood Change."

64. The NRA was quick to distance itself from the militia movement and from any connection to the Oklahoma bombing tragedy. See Tanya K. Metaksa, "Oklahoma City," *American Rifleman* (June 1985): 26; also see Glenn Harlan Reynolds, "Up in Arms about a Revolting Movement," *American Rifleman* (July 1995): 34–35.

65. For example, one poll of Texas residents found that 55 percent of the respondents described their opinion of militia groups as "very unfavorable" and another 21 percent gauged their feeling as "somewhat unfavorable"; see Bob Banta, "Terrorism at Home Alarms Most in Poll," *Austin American-Statesman,* August 21, 1995, p. B-1.

66. "House Republicans Send Gun Control Bill to Floor," *The Gun Owners* 14 (August 15, 1995): 5.

67. "House Republicans Send Gun Control Bill to Floor," p. 5. The internal quote is credited to Republican Georgia Representative Bob Barr.

68. Progun lobbying did result, however, in "watering down" some of the original antiterrorism proposals aimed at controlling guns—such as Representative Charles Schumer's amendment that would have centralized the activities of federal, state, and local police relating to gun crime; see "Congress Passes Government Terror Bill: GOA Lobby Efforts Improve Bill, But Problems Still Remain," *The Gun Owners* 15: 3 (June 14, 1996): 5–6.

69. Jim Wilson, "Handgun Trends after the Crime Bill," *Guns and Ammo* (May 1995): 61–65, 104. The NRA is more optimistic and has advised its members that there is a possibility for the passage of legislation that would repeal the 1994 ban on assault weapons; see "Budget Battle Freezes Gun Bills," NRA Alerts (alerts@NRA.org), December 23, 1995; and "Self-Defense of Paramount Concern in 105th Congress," NRA Alerts (alerts@NRA.org), January 24, 1997.

70. The response distribution for the 1994 General Social Survey question "Do you (or does your husband/wife) go hunting?" is as follows: yes, respondent does (12.9 percent); yes, spouse does (5.2 percent); yes, both do (2.1 percent); and no, neither does (79.6 percent); N = 1,996. According to the NRA, there are 18 million licensed hunters in the United States; see *The NRA Member Guide* (Fairfax, Va.: National Rifle Association, 1992).

71. In 1994, the total population in the United States was 260,651,000—out of which 193,000,000 were age 18 or over; see *Statistical Abstract of the United States, 1995* (Washington, D.C.: Government Printing Office, 1995), 8, 16.

72.   See, for example, Bert Klandermans and Dirk Oegema, "Mobilizing for Peace: The 1983 Peace Demonstration in the Hague," presented at the annual meetings of the American Sociological Association, August 1984.

73.   *Digest of Education Statistics, 1995* (Washington, D.C.: National Center for Education Statistics, 1995), 248.

74.   In the 1990 census, 46.1 percent of the population age 25 and older had at least one year of college; see the RLAT94 data file in Gregg Lee Carter, *Instructor's Manual for Data Happy! Doing Sociology with Student Chip* (Boston: Allyn & Bacon, 1995), 135–36; this file is also available from the Population Studies Center at the University of Michigan in Ann Arbor (contact William H. Frey: billf@ umich.edu). The 1994 General Social Survey found 50.4 percent of the population age 18 and over had one or more years of college education.

75.   See the article "HCI U," in the HCI newsletter *The Outreach* 1 (Summer 1995): 5. For a description of HCI's college campus speaking series, see Jody McPhillips, "Jim and Sarah Brady Further Their Cause of Gun Control," *Providence Journal-Bulletin*, April 21, 1994, p. D-15, and James Brady, "Taking Aim at Guns," *Providence Journal-Bulletin,* April 4, 1992, p. A-12. At the prekindergarten through 12th-grade level, HCI recently began its STAR (Straight Talk about Risks) program. STAR is marketed to teachers for inclusion as part of their health or social science curricula. Materials are available in both English and Spanish and include posters, handouts, bibliographies, videos, and training manuals. Converse, the sneaker manufacturer, is a corporate sponsor of the program, and its logo (a single star) and name appear on all STAR materials. Such corporate and nonprofit agency intrusions into the K–12 educational curricula is a hot topic of concern in the NEA (National Educational Association), the largest teachers' union in the country. The NEA "is urging educators to scrutinize the slick lesson plans—some stamped with company logos—being supplied by businesses, special interests and foreign governments before using them in their classrooms" (Deb Riechmann, "NEA Warns of 'Sponsored' Lessons," *Providence Journal-Bulletin,* January 16, 1996, p. A-2). However, the NEA currently supports STAR.

76.   See the July 13, 1995, letter to the membership signed by Dennis Henigan, HCI's director of legal action.

77.   See, for example, Steven F. Cohn, Steven E. Barkan, and William H. Whitaker, "Activists against Hunger: Membership Character-

istics of a National Social Movement Organization," *Sociological Forum* 8 (March 1993): 113–31. Because many victims of gun violence come from the poorer end of the social class spectrum, many of the middle-class members of HCI might be considered "conscience constituents," a term Michael Harrington uses to describe middle-class liberals with strong sympathies for the underdog groups—see his *Toward a Democratic Left: A Racial Program for a New Majority* (New York: Macmillan, 1968).

78. On its business cards, HCI advertises that it is "One Million Strong"; however, "the method they use for tabulation relies upon contacts with interested parties by any means, not an actual count of dues paying members" (McClure, "An Analysis of Handgun Control, Inc.," p. 3). Of course, this is a highly charged political football, with both sides of the gun control debate leaping at any opportunity to show that the strength of the other side is weakening. The 400,000 dues-paying membership figure was supplied by HCI in January 1996.

79. In their "Handgun Control at a Glimpse," HCI estimated it had "80,000 supporters across the country" in 1980.

80. Anthony Oberschall, *Social Conflict and Social Movements* (Englewood Cliffs, N.J.: Prentice-Hall, 1973), chapter 4.

81. Dallas A. Blanchard, *The Anti-Abortion Movement and the Rise of the Religious Right: From Polite to Fiery Protest* (New York: Twayne Publishers, 1994), 59.

82. Gregg Lee Carter, "What Americans Think about Gun Control," paper presented at the New England Sociological Association Fall Conference, November 5, 1994. The Pearson correlation coefficient between hunters per 1,000 population and percent of adults favoring gun control (as measured by the General Social Survey question "Would you favor or oppose a law which would require a person to obtain a police permit before he or she could buy a gun?") is –.43.

83. Spitzer, *The Politics of Gun Control,* p. 162.

84. See HCI's annual report *Handgun Control Inc., 1995* (Washington, D.C.: Handgun Control Inc., 1995).

85. See chapter 9 ("Demographic Profiles of Gun Owners and NRA Members") in Leddy, *Magnum Force Lobby.*

86. Douglas S. Weil and David Hemenway, "I Am the NRA: An Analysis of a National Random Sample of Gun Owners," *Violence and Victims* 8 (Winter 1993): 353–65.

87. Dennis Henigan, director of HCI's Legal Action Project; quoted remarks taken from his letter to HCI's membership, dated July 13, 1995.

88. David A. Snow, Louis A. Zurcher, and Sheldon Ekland-Olson, "Social Networks and Social Movements: A Microstructural Approach to Differential Recruitment," *American Sociological Review* 45 (December 1980): 787–801.

89. More technically, the movement member can help the potential recruit with the "frame alignment process"—that is, getting the recruit to see his or her "interests, values, and beliefs and SMO [the social-movement organization's] activities, goals, and ideology [as] congruent and complementary. The term *'frame'* ... denote[s] 'schemata of interpretation' that enable individuals 'to locate, perceive, identify, and label' occurrences within their life space and the world at large. By rendering events or occurrences meaningful, frames function to organize experience and guide action, whether individual or collective. So conceptualized, it follows that frame alignment is a necessary condition for movement participation, whatever its nature or intensity." See David A. Snow, E. Burke Rochford Jr., Steven K. Worden, and Robert D. Benford, "Frame Alignment Processes, Micromobilization, and Movement Participation," *American Sociological Review* 51 (August 1986): 464.

90. Personal interview with Jeanne Shields; also see Shields, *Guns Don't Die—People Do,* p. 96.

91. "STOP Doc Goes All Out to Keep Kids Safe," *Center to Prevent Handgun Violence Rx for Gun Violence* 3 (Summer 1995): 4.

92. McAdam, McCarthy, and Zald, "Social Movements," p. 708.

93. *Handgun Control Inc. 1995* annual report.

94. Richard T. LaPiere, "Attitude vs. Actions," *Social Forces* 13 (December 1934): 230–37.

95. *The Outreach,* p. 5.

96. Personal interview with Jeanne Shields; also see Shields, *Guns Don't Die—People Do,* pp. 134–44.

97. As quoted in Shields, *Guns Don't Die—People Do,* p. 135.

98. *The Outreach,* p. 3.

99. *The Outreach,* p. 5.

100. Wayne King, "Weapon Used by Deranged Man Easy to Buy," *New York Times,* January 19, 1989, p. B-6.

101. Personal interviews at HCI headquarters in Washington, D.C., August 19, 1995.

102. Robert C. Mitchell, "National Environmental Lobbies and the Apparent Illogic of Collective Action," in *Collective Decision-*

Making Applications from Public Choice Theory, ed. Clifford S. Russell (Baltimore: Johns Hopkins University Press, 1979), 87–121.

103. Liberal tendencies in the media are analyzed in Robert Lichter, Linda Lichter, and Stanley Rothman, *Center for Media and Public Affairs, 1991 Report.*

104. In a letter from Larry Pratt to the membership of the Gun Owners of America that accompanied the organization's December 1995 issue of its newsletter, *The Gun Owner.*

105. "Momentum against Guns" (editorial), *Providence Journal-Bulletin,* December 15, 1993. Similar pro–gun control/anti-NRA editorials and opinion/editorial essays appear in the following issues of this newspaper: May 6, 1994 (J. Joseph Garrahy, B. Jae Clanton, Alan Hassenfeld, and Gail Borges, "Let's Protect Kids from Guns." p. A-15); September 9, 1993 (Leonard Larsen, "Stop the Killing—and the Gun-Nut Lobby"); April 25, 1993 ("A Harder Line on Guns," p. A-10).

106. "Keep Pushing on Gun Control" (editorial), *New York Times,* September 6, 1994, p. A-18. Similar pro–gun control/anti-NRA editorials appear in the following issues of this newspaper: May 20, 1995 ("Wayne LaPierre on the Ropes," p. 22); March 21, 1995 ("Mr. Dole's Transparent Tactics," p. A-20); May 21, 1994 ("Curing the Handgun Epidemic," p. 20); May 3, 1994 ("Demand Action on Assault Weapons," p. A-22); April 26, 1994 ("The NRA's Indecent Attack," p. A-22); and March 2, 1994 ("Another Blow to the NRA," p. A-14).

107. The NRA maintains that the amendment protects the rights of private citizens to keep and bear arms, while HCI holds that it protects the rights of states to have their own militias—see chapter 2 for analysis of the debate over the Second Amendment.

108. This advertisement is reproduced in *Legal Action Report* 10 (July 1995): 3, available from HCI (1225 I Street NW, #1100, Washington, D.C. 20005).

109. "Campaign to Protect Sane Gun Laws," *The Outreach,* p. 1.

110. "Campaign to Protect Sane Gun Laws," p. 1.

111. Personal interview with Edward Welles.

112. See Herbert H. Haines, "Black Radicalization and the Funding of Civil Rights: 1957–1970," *Social Problems* 32 (February 1984): 31–43.

113. Philanthropists making large (more than $10,000) contributions to HCI include the Columbia Foundation, the Public Welfare Foundation, the Shelly and Donald Rubin Foundation, the Scherman

Foundation, and the Sidney Stern Memorial Trust. See *Rx for Violence,* p. 3.

114.   See Carol A. Schwartz and Rebecca L. Turner (eds.), *Encyclopedia of Associations, 1995, Volume 1: National Organizations of the U.S., Part 2* (Washington, D.C.: Gale Research, 1995), 2008–9.

115.   Sugarmann, *NRA: Money, Firepower, Fear,* pp. 254–62.

116.   As quoted in Sugarmann, *NRA: Money, Firepower, Fear,* p. 189.

117.   *Center to Prevent Handgun Violence 1993–94 Annual Report* (Washington, D.C.: Center to Prevent Handgun Violence, 1995), 5–6.

118.   *Center to Prevent Handgun Violence 1993–94 Annual Report,* pp. 7–8.

119.   C. Everett Koop and George D. Lundberg, "Violence in America: A Public Health Emergency—Time to Bite the Bullet Back," *Journal of the American Medical Association* 267 (June 10, 1992): 3075–76; Yank D. Coble Jr., et al., "Assault Weapons as a Public Health Hazard in the United States: Council on Scientific Affairs Report," *Journal of the American Medical Association* 267 (June 10, 1992): 3067–70.

120.   Miguel A. Faria Jr., "On Public Health and Gun Control," *Journal of the Medical Association of Georgia* 84 (June 1995): 251–52.

121.   James Mason, "From the Assistant Secretary for Health, U.S. Public Health Service," *Journal of the American Medical Association* 267 (June 10, 1992): 3003; Antonia C. Novello, John Shosky, and Robert Froehlke, "From the Surgeon General, U.S. Public Health Service," *Journal of the American Medical Association* 267 (June 10, 1992): 3007.

122.   Mark L. Rosenberg, Patrick W. O'Carroll, and Keenth E. Powell, "Let's Be Clear: Violence Is a Public Health Problem," *Journal of the American Medical Association* 267 (June 10, 1992): 3071.

123.   Koop and Lundberg, "Violence in America: A Public Health Emergency—Time to Bite the Bullet Back," p. 3076.

124.   For example, see "Two Challenges to Federal Assault Weapon Ban Dismissed," *Legal Action Report* 10 (July 1995): 5.

125.   "Victory Achieved in Round One of 101 California Street Litigation," *Legal Action Report* 10 (July 1995): 1.

126.   "Center Files 'Personalized' Gun Lawsuit against Beretta," *Legal Action Report* 10 (July 1995): 5.

127.   Personal interview with Edward Welles.

128.   William Gamson, *The Strategy of Social Protest,* 2d ed. (Belmont, Calif.: Wadsworth, 1990), 45–46.

129.   Shields, *Guns Don't Die—People Do,* p. 133.

130.   Spitzer, *The Politics of Gun Control,* pp. 125, 169–70. This section will concentrate on the NRA, even though several other smaller organizations are part of the countermovement. These organizations—most notably the Gun Owners of America (GOA) and the Citizens Committee for the Right to Keep and Bear Arms (CCRKBA)—serve as *radical flanks* (see figure 5.3). Having extremist allies can benefit a more moderate SMO, ultimately giving it more influence than it would have had otherwise. GOA and CCRKBA serve this role for the NRA. For example, the NRA-supported H.R. 1488 (designed to repeal the 1994 assault-weapons ban) is characterized as a "Trojan Horse in the pro-gun community" by the GOA, while conservative Republican Bob Dole, an NRA favored son, is described as heading "the betrayal of gun owners ... in the Senate" (see GOA's newsletter *The Gun Owners* 14 [August 1995]: 2, 7). Congressional representatives opposed to gun control are more prone to build relationships with the NRA because of its less vitriolic attitude.

Although the NRA works with GOA and CCRKBA from time to time on Capitol Hill, the resentment of the smaller organizations is sometimes apparent, as in GOA Executive Director Larry Pratt's allusion to the NRA as a "certain gun rights leader" that is willing to support the "throwing of parliamentary hand grenades" by "GOP leaders" in the path of legislators wanting to repeal the 1994 assault-weapons ban ("GOA Members Make Their Voices Heard on Capitol Hill," *The Gun Owners* 14 [December 1995]: 1–2; in the same issue, the GOA advertises itself as "the only no compromise gun lobby in Washington," p. 1). The tension between the NRA and its smaller allies is sometimes expressed by the dominant organization, too: Sugarmann quotes NRA lobbyist James Jay Baker characterizing CCRKBA and similar progun splinter group lobbyists as "those nuts" (see *NRA: Money, Firepower, Fear,* p. 130).

131.   *NRA-ILA Fact Sheet* (Fairfax, Va.: National Rifle Association, June 1994); the NRA claims to have a balanced budget and $52 million in cash and investments, plus some $25 million in other net tangible assets (see Wayne LaPierre, "Standing Guard," *American Rifleman,* September 1995, p. 7).

132. For detailed accountings of these NRA successes, see Davidson, *Under Fire;* Leddy, *Magnum Force Lobby;* Shields, *Guns Don't Die—People Do;* and Sugarmann, *NRA: Money, Firepower, Fear.*

133. Wayne LaPierre, "NRA Priority Express" (letter to the membership), July 1995; Craig D. Sandler and Ron Keysor, "NRA and Law Enforcement—Ties That Bind," *American Rifleman* (August 1995): 40–41, 62–63.

134. *Guns, Bias, and the Evening News* (Fairfax, Va.: National Rifle Association, 1994).

135. Although a 1.2-billion-dollar industry in the United States, firearms manufacturers are relatively weak players in the gun control debate. Sugarmann and others argue that the industry has not had to become politically active because the NRA acts, in effect, as its voice (in return, industry ads placed in NRA publications produce millions of dollars in revenue—for example, $7.5 million in 1990—for the organization; manufacturers also insert NRA membership applications in their packaging); see B. Drummond Ayres Jr., "Gun Maker on Mayhem: That Is Not Our Doing," *New York Times,* March 19, 1994, p. 8; Spitzer, *The Politics of Gun Control,* pp. 103–5; and Sugarmann, *NRA: Money, Firepower, Fear,* especially chapter 4. Only the recent set of HCI-inspired lawsuits against gun manufacturers—such as Beretta and Intratec (discussed earlier)—has forced them to become active participants in the gun control debate. Not unexpectedly, gun manufacturers and dealers draw no connection between their wares and the amount of gun violence in U.S. society: "To blame the gun for its misuse is to avoid dealing with the real issue.... [T]he issue is poverty, drugs, and jobs" (Ronald E. Stilwell, president, Colt Manufacturing). "We're the excuse for the failure of the liberal courts, for the lawyers who screwed up the system, for the people who don't want to make hard decisions" (Andrew Mochan, president, National Association of Federally Licensed Firearms Dealers). See Erik Eckholm, "Ailing Gun Industry Confronts Outrage Over Glut of Violence," *New York Times,* March 8, 1992, p. 1.

136. As quoted in Davidson, *Under Fire,* p. 39.

137. Laura I. Langbein and Mark A. Lotwis, "The Political Efficacy of Lobbying and Money: Gun Control in the U.S. House, 1986," *Legislative Studies Quarterly* 15 (August 1990): 413–40; Laura I. Langbein, "PACs, Lobbies, and Political Conflict: The Case of Gun Control," *Public Choice* 77 (November 1993): 573–94.

138.　See Davidson, *Under Fire,* chapter 6; Sherrill, *Saturday Night Special,* pp. 197–202; and Sugarmann, *NRA: Money, Firepower, Fear,* chapter 8.

139.　Sherrill, *The Saturday Night Special,* pp. 198–99.

140.　Davidson, *Under Fire,* p. 145.

141.　See Pat Dunham, *Electoral Behavior in the United States* (Englewood Cliffs, N.J.: Prentice-Hall, 1991), especially pp. 190–94.

142.　Everett Carll Ladd, "The 1994 Congressional Elections: The Postindustrial Realignment Continues," *Political Science Quarterly* 110 (Spring 1995): 14–15. The Republicans experienced a net gain of 52 House seats, 9 Senate seats, 14 governorships, and 18 state legislative houses.

143.　Ladd, "The 1994 Congressional Elections: The Postindustrial Realignment Continues," pp. 8, 9.

144.　Richard E. Cohen, "NRA Draws a Bead on Incumbents," *National Journal* 24 (September 19, 1992): 2134.

145.　See Eckholm, "Ailing Gun Industry Confronts Outrage over Glut of Violence," p. 1; and Marianne W. Zawitz, *Guns Used in Crime* (Washington, D.C.: Bureau of Justice Statistics, U.S. Department of Justice, July 1995, NCJ-148201), 2–3.

Bibliography

The literature on gun control is vast and highly biased—even when written by supposedly dispassionate scholars. Academicians and popular writers alike almost always begin their individual studies with either a pro- or antigun slant, and then proceed to line up the evidence to correspond with it—ignoring or discounting or minimizing any studies that do not fit. The works listed here are the most important in the field; however, I alert the reader to their pro- or antigun prejudices.

Chapter One
For both the pro- and antigun interpretations of U.S. and cross-national crime and violence as a function of gun prevalence, see the various articles in Charles P. Cozic (ed.), *Gun Control* (San Diego, Calif.: Greenhaven Press, 1992), and in Lee Nisbet (ed.), *The Gun Control Debate: You Decide* (Buffalo, N.Y.: Prometheus Books, 1990). Progun lawyer–writer David B. Kopel's analyses of gun violence in the United States compared to Great Britain, Canada, and Japan lead him to conclude that the key explanation of a nation's violence should be sought in culture, not gun availability; see his *Gun Control in Great Britain: Saving Lives or Constricting Liberty?* (Chicago: Office of International Criminal Justice, University of Illinois, 1992) and his *The Samurai, the Mountie, and the Cowboy: Should America Adopt the Gun Controls of Other Democracies?* (Buffalo, N.Y.: Prometheus Books, 1992). Kopel's similarly progun anthology, *Guns: Who Should Have Them?* (Amherst, N.Y.: Prometheus Books, 1995), contains U.S. and cross-national analyses contending that only a weak—or even nonexistent—link exists between gun prevalence and crime, violence, suicide, or accidents. In contrast, Martin Killias argues that there are strong links between

cross-national homicide/suicide rates and gun availability in his "International Correlations between Gun Ownership and Rates of Homicide and Suicide" (*Canadian Medical Association Journal*, 148 [May 15, 1993]: 1721–25). Killias's gun data are taken from one of the best-known and most often used sources of cross-national crime data, *Experiences of Crime across the World: Key Findings from the 1989 International Crime Survey* (Boston: Kluwer Law and Taxation Publishers, 1991)—authored by Jan J.M. van Dijk, Pat Mayhew, and Killias himself.

Analyses of U.S. data on the gun availability/gun violence relationship from a basically antigun stand include Geoffrey Canada, *Fist, Stick, Knife, Gun: A Personal History of Violence in America* (Boston: Beacon Press, 1995); Philip J. Cook and Mark H. Moore, "Gun Control," in *Crime,* ed. James Q. Wilson and Joan Petersilia (San Francisco: Institute for Contemporary Studies, 1995), 267–94; Erik Larson, *Lethal Passage: How the Travels of a Single Handgun Expose the Roots of America's Gun Crisis* (New York: Crown Publishers, 1994); Landis MacKellar and Machiko Yanagishita, *Homicide in the United States: Who's at Risk?* (Washington, D.C.: Population Reference Bureau, 1995); and Albert J. Reiss Jr. and Jeffrey A. Roth (eds.), *Understanding and Preventing Violence* (Washington, D.C.: National Academy Press, 1993, chapter 6). Similar analyses, but from a progun stance, are the classic studies of James D. Wright and his colleagues published as *Armed and Considered Dangerous: A Survey of Felons and Their Firearms* (New York: Aldine de Gruyter, 1986)—written with Peter H. Rossi; and *Under the Gun: Weapons, Crime, and Violence in America* (New York: Aldine de Gruyter, 1983)—coauthored with Rossi and Kathleen Daly. Finally, progun author Gary Kleck's *Point Blank: Guns and Violence in America* (New York: Aldine de Gruyter, 1991) contains comprehensive analyses of the relationship between gun availability and gun violence (crime and suicide)—all of which show little or no statistical significance.

Chapter Two

Virtually all recent scholarly analyses of the Second Amendment have been motivated by the gun control debate. Both pro- and antigun stances are represented by the essays in Robert Emmet Long (ed.), *Gun Control: The Reference Shelf,* Vol. 60, No. 6 (New York: H.W. Wilson, 1989). Progun authors have history on their side when they argue that the framers of the Bill of Rights intended the Second Amendment to guarantee an *individual*—and not just a collective—right. Among the most readable of these are Clayton E. Cramer, *For the Defense of Themselves: The Original Intent and Judicial Interpretation of the Right to Keep and Bear Arms* (Westport, Conn.: Praeger, 1994); Stephen P. Halbrook, *A Right to Bear Arms: State and Federal Bills of Rights and Constitutional Guarantees* (Westport, Conn.: Greenwood Press, 1989); David T. Hardy, *Origins and Development of the Second Amendment* (Chino Valley, Ariz.: Blacksmith Publishers, 1986); Joyce Lee Malcolm, *To Keep and Bear Arms: The Origins of an Anglo-American Right* (Cambridge, Mass.: Harvard University Press, 1994); and the various authors in the *Tennessee Law Review: A Second Amendment Symposium Issue* (Vol. 62, No. 3, Spring 1995). Hardy's work contains mainly original sources and has the least amount of interpretation.

Antigun authors emphasize that the original aim of the Second Amendment was to guarantee the right of the states to form their own militias and that no personal right to keep and bear arms was ever intended. Further, these authors argue that even if the original aim were to guarantee the rights of individuals, the courts and legislatures of the states and of the federal government have never felt the need to be in lockstep with such an interpretation—that, indeed, they have regularly infringed on the right to keep and bear arms by way of a host of gun regulations and rulings. The most readable progun books on the Second Amendment are Dennis A. Henigan, E. Bruce Nicholson, and David Hemenway, *Guns and the Constitution: The Myth of the Second Amendment Protection for Firearms in America* (Northampton, Mass.: Aletheia Press, 1995), and Warren Freedman, *The Privilege to Keep and Bear Arms: The Second Amendment and Its Interpretation* (New York: Quorum Books, 1990).

Antigun author James Coates's *Armed and Dangerous* (New York: Hill and Wang, 1995) provides one of the few analyses of the private militia movement. The 1995 Oklahoma City bombing tragedy will surely stimulate more research and publication on this topic in the near future.

Chapter Three

Lee Kennett and James LaVerne Anderson's *The Gun in America: The Origins of a National Dilemma* (Westport, Conn.: Greenwood Press, 1975) is the best overall description of the role of guns in American history. Very good histories of frontier America that include the role of firearms can be found in Ray Allen Billington, *America's Frontier Her-*

itage (New York: Holt, Rinehart & Winston, 1966); Richard J. Hofstadter and Michael Wallace, *American Violence: A Documentary History* (New York: Alfred A. Knopf, 1970); W. Eugene Hollon, *Frontier Violence: Another Look* (New York: Oxford University Press, 1974); and the various articles in Ted Robert Gurr (ed.), *Violence in America, Volume 1: The History of Crime* (Newbury Park, Calif.: Sage Publications, 1989). All of these historical works are among the least biased in the gun debate literature, though a subtle antigun stance is sometimes apparent.

Chapter Four

American attitudes on guns greatly favor the advocates of gun control. Readable analyses of these data by antigun authors include Tom Smith, "The 75% Solution: An Analysis of the Structure of Attitudes on Gun Control, 1959–1977," *Journal of Criminal Law and Criminology* 71 (1980): 300–16, and David W. Moore and Frank Newport, "Public Strongly Favors Stricter Gun Control Laws," *The Gallup Poll Monthly* (January 1994): 18–24.

Progun author Gary Kleck's reexamination of public-opinion studies stresses that they tell us little about the actual feelings of people; see his *Point Blank* (cited earlier). James D. Wright reaches a similar conclusion in his "Public Opinion and Gun Control," *Annals of the American Academy of Political and Social Science* 453 (May 1981): 24–39. For an objective analysis on how public opinion affects the political process more generally, see Robert S. Erikson, Norman R. Luttbeg, and Kent L. Tedin, *American Public Opinion: Its Origins, Content, and Impact*, 4th ed. (New York: Macmillan, 1991).

Chapter Five

For generally antigun analyses of the gun control debate as it is played out in American society and politics, see Wilbur Edel, *Gun Control: Threat to Liberty or Defense against Anarchy?* (Westport, Conn.: Praeger, 1995); Gerald D. Robin, *Violent Crime and Gun Control* (Cincinnati: Anderson Publishing Co., 1991); and the various articles in *The Annals of the American Academy of Political and Social Science* 453 (May 1981).

For progun descriptions of how the NRA and its allies work the political system to achieve their aims, see Edward F. Leddy, *Magnum Force Lobby: The National Rifle Association Fights Gun Control* (Lanham, Md.: University Press of America, 1987); Wayne R. LaPierre,

Guns, Crime, and Freedom (Washington, D.C.: Regnery Publishing, 1994); and almost any issue of the NRA's monthly publication *American Rifleman.* LaPierre is the NRA's chief national spokesperson. For antigun descriptions of the same topic, see Osha Gray Davidson, *Under Fire: The NRA and the Battle for Gun Control* (New York: Henry Holt, 1993); Robert Sherrill, *The Saturday Night Special* (New York: Charterhouse, 1972); Pete Shields, *Guns Don't Die—People Do* (New York: Arbor House, 1981); Robert J. Spitzer, *The Politics of Gun Control* (Chatham, N.J.: Chatham House, 1995); and Josh Sugarmann, *NRA: Money, Firepower, Fear* (Washington, D.C.: National Press Books, 1992). Shields (deceased in 1993) was chair of Handgun Control Incorporated, while Sugarmann is executive director of the gun control advocacy group, Violence Policy Center.

For more objective analyses on how pressure groups influence Congress and the political process more generally, see Jeffrey H. Birnbaum, *The Lobbyists: How Influence Peddlers Get Their Way in Washington* (New York: Times Books, 1992); Leroy N. Rieselbach, *Congressional Politics: The Evolving Legislative System*, 2d ed. (Boulder, Colo.: Westview Press, 1995); Bruce C. Wolpe, *Lobbying Congress: How the System Works* (Washington, D.C.: Congressional Quarterly, 1990); and the various articles in Allan J. Cigler and Burdett A. Loomis (eds.), *Interest Group Politics,* 2d ed. (Washington, D.C.: Congressional Quarterly, 1986). Finally, for a somewhat dated but still highly useful summary of social-movement theory, see Doug McAdam, John D. McCarthy, and Mayer N. Zald, "Social Movements," in *Handbook of Sociology,* ed. Neil J. Smelser (Newbury Park, Calif.: Sage Publications, 1988), 695–737.

Index

The Author

Gregg Lee Carter is professor of sociology at Bryant College in Smith-field, Rhode Island. He earned his Ph.D. at Columbia University, where his dissertation was on the African-American rioting of the 1960s. His articles on the rioting and other areas of collective behavior have appeared in the *Journal of Conflict Resolution, Sociological Focus, Sociological Forum, Sociological Inquiry,* and *The Sociological Quarterly.* He is also the author of *Empirical Approaches to Sociology* (Allyn & Bacon, 1998), *How to Manage Conflict in the Organization* (American Management Association, 1994), *Doing Sociology with Student Chip* (Allyn & Bacon, 1998), *Analyzing Contemporary Social Issues* (Allyn & Bacon, 1996), and *Perspectives on Current Social Problems* (Allyn & Bacon, 1997). His current research is on the sociology of working women. Professor Carter is past president of the New England Sociological Association (1994–1995) and has been an associate editor of *Teaching Sociology* (1993–1996).

The Editor

Robert D. Benford received his Ph.D. from the University of Texas at Austin in 1987 and is associate professor of sociology at the University of Nebraska–Lincoln. His published works include *The Nuclear Cage* (with Lester Kurtz and Jennifer Turpin) and numerous articles and book chapters on social movements, nuclear politics, war and peace museums, environmental controversies, and qualitative research methods. His current research focuses on the linkages between the social construction of movement discourse, collective identity, and collective memory.